An Introduction to
SolidWorks Flow Simulation 2009

John E. Matsson, Ph.D.

ISBN: 978-1-58503-543-4

SDC
PUBLICATIONS

Schroff Development Corporation

www.schroff.com

Schroff Development Corporation
P.O. Box 1334
Mission KS 66222
(913) 262-2664
www.**schroff**.com

Publisher: Stephen Schroff

Trademarks and Disclaimer

SolidWorks® is a registered trademark of Dassault Systemes SolidWorks Corporation. Microsoft Windows® and its family products are registered trademarks of the Microsoft Corporation.

Every effort has been made to provide an accurate text. The author and the manufacturers shall not be held liable for any parts developed with this book or held responsible for any inaccuracies or errors that appear in the book.

Copyright

Examination Copies

Books received as examination copies are for review purposes only and may not be made available for student use. Resale of examination copes is prohibited.

Electronic Files

Any electronic files associated with this book are licensed to the original user only. These files may not be transferred to any other party.

Acknowledgements

I would like to thank Stephen Schroff and Mary Schmidt of Schroff Development Corporation for their help in preparing this book for publication. I would also like to thank Oral Roberts University and the School of Science and Engineering for providing support during my sabbatical leave. I dedicate this book to my wife Åsa and my children Josefin, Kristoffer and Madeleine for their love, patience and support.

About the Cover

The cover is showing a surface plot and a cut plot of the circumferential velocity component in Taylor-Couette flow between two rotating cylinders. This flow is studied in Chapter 5 Rayleigh-Bénard Convection and Taylor-Couette flow.

About the Author

Dr. John Matsson is an Associate Professor of Mechanical Engineering and Chair of the Engineering, Physics and Physical Science Department at Oral Roberts University in Tulsa, Oklahoma. He earned M.S. and Ph.D. degrees from the Royal Institute of Technology in Stockholm, Sweden in 1988 and 1994, respectively and completed postdoctoral work at the Norwegian University of Science and Technology in Trondheim, Norway. His teaching areas include Applied Thermodynamics, Experimental Methods, Finite Element Methods, Fluid Mechanics, Heat Transfer, Manufacturing Processes and Principles of Design. He is the Chair of the American Society of Mechanical Engineers ASME Mid-Continent Section, senior member of the American Institute of Aeronautics and Astronautics (AIAA) and also a member of the American Physical Society (APS), the American Society of Engineering Education (ASEE), the American Society of Heating, Refrigerating and Air-Conditioning Engineers (ASHRAE) and the Society of Manufacturing Engineers (SME). Please contact the author jmatsson@oru.edu with any comments, questions, or suggestions on this book.

Files needed for this book can be downloaded from:

www.schroff.com/resources

Notes:

Table of Contents

Chapter 1   Introduction

SolidWorks Flow Simulation Introduction

SolidWorks Flow Simulation 2009 is a fluid flow analysis add-in package that is available for SolidWorks in order to obtain solutions to the full Navier-Stokes equations that govern the motion of fluids. Other packages that can be added to SolidWorks include SolidWorks Motion and SolidWorks Simulation. A fluid flow analysis using Flow Simulation involves a number of basic steps that are shown in the following flowchart in figure 1.1.

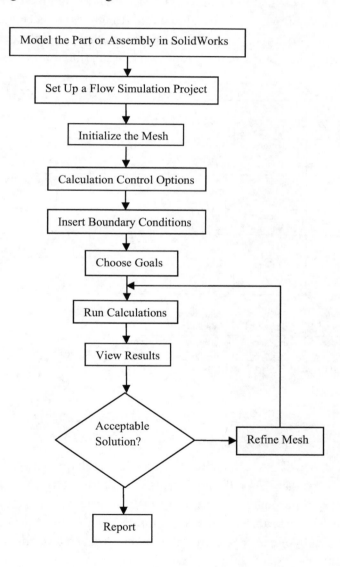

Figure 1.1 Flowchart for fluid flow analysis using SolidWorks Flow Simulation

Setting Up a SolidWorks Flow Simulation Project

The process of setting up a Flow Simulation project includes the following general setting steps in order: choosing the analysis type, selecting a fluid and a solid and settings of wall condition and initial and ambient conditions. Any fluid flow problem that is solved using Flow Simulation must be categorized as either internal bounded or external unbounded flow. Examples of internal flows include flows bounded by walls such as pipe- and channel flows, heat exchangers and obstruction flow meters. External flow examples include flows around airfoils and fuselages of airplanes and fluid flow related to different sports such as flows over golf balls, baseballs and soccer balls. Furthermore, during the project setup process a fluid is chosen as belonging to one of the following six categories: gas, liquid, non-Newtonian liquid, compressible liquid, real gas or steam. Physical features that can be taken into account include heat conduction in solids, radiation, time-varying flows, gravity and rotation. Roughness of surfaces can be specified and different thermal conditions for walls can be chosen including adiabatic walls or specified heat flux, heat transfer rate or wall temperature. For a more complete list of possible settings, see table 1.1.

General Settings					
Analysis type	Internal	External			
Physical Features	Heat Conduction in Solids	Radiation	Time-dependence	Gravity	Rotation
Fluids	Gases	Liquids	Non-Newtonian Liquids	Compressible Liquids	Real Gases	Steam
Flow Types	Laminar	Laminar and Turbulent	Turbulent		
Solids	Alloys	Glasses and Minerals	Metals	Non-Isotropic Solids	Polymers	Semi-conductors
Wall Thermal Condition	Adiabatic Wall	Heat Flux	Heat Transfer Rate	Temperature	
Thermodynamic Parameters	Pressure	Temperature	Density		
Velocity Parameters	Velocity in X direction	Velocity in Y direction	Velocity in Z direction		
Turbulence Parameters	Turbulence Intensity	Turbulence Length	Turbulence Energy	Turbulence Dissipation	

Table 1.1 List of different general settings in SolidWorks Flow Simulation

Meshing in SolidWorks Flow Simulation

The SolidWorks Flow Simulation mesh consists of cells in the form of rectangular parallelepipeds. The Flow Simulation mesh can contain basic cells of three different types: fluid cells, partial cells and solid cells see figure 1.2. Basic cells can be split during the process of refinement. During refinement, each basic cell is split in eight smaller cells with the same volume, see figure 1.2. Therefore, the volume of each refined cell is only 1/8 of the original volume. There are a maximum of seven refinement levels that can be set in the calculation control options. A table of the different available mesh settings is summarized in table 1.2. An essential part of any computational study of fluid flows is to vary the density of the computational mesh and study whether the solution converges as the mesh is refined. However, it should be remembered that a fine mesh in fluid flow simulations may require a substantial amount of RAM and that calculations can take a very long time to reach convergence.

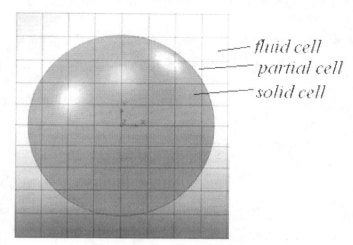

Figure 1.2 Different types of mesh cells

 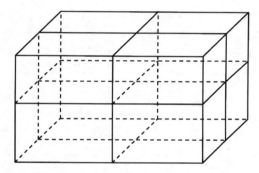

Figure 1.3 Refinement of a rectangular parallelepiped

Mesh Settings				
Automatic Settings	*Level of Initial Mesh*	*Minimum Gap Size*	*Minimum Wall Thickness*	
Manual Settings	*Basic Mesh*	*Solid/Fluid Interface*	*Refining Cells*	*Narrow Channels*
	Number of Cells per X <1001	Small Solid Features Refinement Level < 8	All Cells	Number of Cells
	Number of Cells per Y <1001	Curvature Refinement Level < 8	Fluid Cells	Refinement Level
	Number of Cells per Z <1001	Tolerance Refinement Level < 8	Partial Cells	Minimum Height
			Solid Cells	Maximum Height

Table 1.2 List of mesh settings in SolidWorks Flow Simulation

There are also a number of six control planes available in Flow Simulation that can be used to optimally contract or expand the mesh in order to assure that details and features of the geometry will be captured by the computational mesh.

The computational mesh is recommended to be constructed in the following order:

a) Start by using the automatic mesh setting. Set the minimum gap size and minimum wall thickness to appropriate values.
b) Turn off automatic settings and set your own basic mesh values with both the small solid features refinement level and the curvature refinement level set to zero. Disable the narrow channel refinement.
c) Increase both the small solid features refinement level and the curvature refinement level in steps and enable the narrow channel refinement.

Calculation Control Options

There are a number of ways in which you can control your calculations, see table 1.3. As shown in the table the finishing conditions include refinement number, iterations, calculation time and travels. Travel is defined as the number of iterations related to the propagation of a perturbation through the computational domain. In the value drop down box of the calculation control options it is possible to choose whether calculations will stop when one of the finishing conditions is satisfied or when all of them are satisfied. The maximum number of travels depends on the specific goals that are used in the calculations, result resolution level and the type of problem that is studied.

Calculation Control Options			
Finish Conditions	*Saving*	*Refinement*	*Advanced*
Minimum Refinement Number	Save Before Refinement	Disabled	Flow Freezing
Maximum Iterations	Periodic Saving	Level = 1 - 7	Notify when calculation is finished
Maximum Calculation Time	Tabular Saving		
Maximum Travels			

Table 1.3 List of mesh settings in SolidWorks Flow Simulation

Inserting Boundary Conditions

Boundary conditions are required for both the inflow and outflow faces of internal flow regions with the exception of enclosures subjected to natural convection. Visualization of boundary conditions can be shown with arrows of different colors indicating the type and direction of the boundary condition. The boundary conditions are divided in three different types: flow openings, pressure openings and walls, see table 1.4.

Boundary Conditions								
Flow Openings	Inlet Mass Flow	Inlet Volume Flow	Inlet Velocity	Inlet Mach Number	Outlet Mass Flow	Outlet Volume Flow	Outlet Velocity	Outlet Mach Number
Pressure Openings	Environment Pressure	Static Pressure	Total Pressure					
Wall	Real Wall	Ideal Wall						

Table 1.4 List of available boundary conditions in SolidWorks Flow Simulation

Each boundary condition has a number of parameters related to it that can be set to different values. The available parameters for each boundary condition are shown in table 1.5.

Boundary Conditions

	Flow Parameters	Thermodynamic Parameters	Turbulence Parameters	Boundary Layer	Wall Parameters	Wall Motion	Options
Inlet Mass Flow	√	√	√	√			√
Inlet Volume Flow	√	√	√	√			√
Inlet Velocity	√	√	√	√			√
Inlet Mach Number	√	√	√	√			√
Outlet Mass Flow	√						√
Outlet Volume Flow	√						√
Outlet Velocity	√						√
Outlet Mach Number	√						√
Environment Pressure		√	√	√			√
Static Pressure		√	√	√			√
Total Pressure		√	√	√			√
Real Wall					√	√	√
Ideal Wall							√

Table 1.5 List of available parameters for different boundary conditions in SolidWorks Flow Simulation

The flow parameter depends on the boundary condition but includes velocity, Mach number and mass and volume flow rate. The direction of the flow vector can be specified as normal to the face, as swirl or as a 3D vector. The thermodynamic parameters include temperature and pressure. For the turbulence parameters you can choose between specifying the turbulence intensity and length or the turbulence energy and dissipation (k-ε turbulence model). The boundary layer is set to either laminar or turbulent. You can also specify velocity and thermal boundary layer thickness for the inlet velocity boundary condition as well as specify the core velocity and temperature. For the real wall boundary condition you can specify the wall roughness together with wall temperature and heat transfer coefficient. The real wall also has an option for motion in the form of translational or angular velocity.

Choosing Goals

Goals are criteria used to stop the iterative solution process. The goals are chosen from the physical parameters of interest to the user of Flow Simulation. The use of goals minimizes errors in the calculated parameters and shortens the total solution time for the solver. There are five different types of goals: global goals, point goals, surface goals, volume goals and equation goals. The global goal is based on parameter values determined everywhere in the flow field whereas a point goal is related to a specific point inside the computational domain. Surface goals are determined on specific surfaces and volume goals are determined within a specific subset of the computational domain as specified by the user.

Finally, equation goals are defined by mathematical expressions. Table 1.6 is showing 48 different parameters that can be chosen by the different types of goals.

GG: Global Goal, SG: Surface Goal, VG: Volume Goal					PG: Point Goal
Parameter	Minimum	Average	Maximum	Bulk Average	Value
Static Pressure	GG, SG, VG	GG, SG, VG	GG, SG, VG	GG, SG, VG	PG
Total Pressure	GG, SG, VG	GG, SG, VG	GG, SG, VG	GG, SG, VG	PG
Dynamic Pressure	GG, SG, VG	GG, SG, VG	GG, SG, VG	GG, SG, VG	PG
Temperature of Fluid	GG, SG, VG	GG, SG, VG	GG, SG, VG	GG, SG, VG	PG
Density	GG, SG, VG	GG, SG, VG	GG, SG, VG	GG, SG, VG	PG
Mass Flow Rate			GG, SG		
Mass in Volume			VG		
Volume Flow Rate			SG		
Velocity	GG, SG, VG	GG, SG, VG	GG, SG, VG	GG, SG, VG	PG
X-Component of Velocity	GG, SG, VG	GG, SG, VG	GG, SG, VG	GG, SG, VG	PG
Y-Component of Velocity	GG, SG, VG	GG, SG, VG	GG, SG, VG	GG, SG, VG	PG
Z-Component of Velocity	GG, SG, VG	GG, SG, VG	GG, SG, VG	GG, SG, VG	PG
Mach Number	GG, SG, VG	GG, SG, VG	GG, SG, VG	GG, SG, VG	PG
Turbulent Viscosity	GG, SG, VG	GG, SG, VG	GG, SG, VG	GG, SG, VG	PG
Turbulent Time	GG, SG, VG	GG, SG, VG	GG, SG, VG	GG, SG, VG	PG
Turbulent Length	GG, SG, VG	GG, SG, VG	GG, SG, VG	GG, SG, VG	PG
Turbulent Intensity	GG, SG, VG	GG, SG, VG	GG, SG, VG	GG, SG, VG	PG
Turbulent Energy	GG, SG, VG	GG, SG, VG	GG, SG, VG	GG, SG, VG	PG
Turbulent Dissipation	GG, SG, VG	GG, SG, VG	GG, SG, VG	GG, SG, VG	PG
Heat Flux	GG, SG	GG, SG	GG, SG		
X-Component of Heat Flux	GG, SG	GG, SG	GG, SG		
Y-Component of Heat Flux	GG, SG	GG, SG	GG, SG		
Z-Component of Heat Flux	GG, SG	GG, SG	GG, SG		
Heat Transfer Rate			GG, SG		
X-Component of Heat Transfer Rate			GG, SG		
Y-Component of Heat Transfer Rate			GG, SG		
Z-Component of Heat Transfer Rate			GG, SG		
Normal Force			GG, SG		
X-Component of Normal Force			GG, SG		
Y-Component of Normal Force			GG, SG		
Z-Component of Normal Force			GG, SG		
Force			GG, SG		
X-Component of Force			GG, SG		
Y-Component of Force			GG, SG		
Z-Component of Force			GG, SG		
Shear Force			GG, SG		
X-Component of Shear Force			GG, SG		
Y-Component of Shear Force			GG, SG		
Z-Component of Shear Force			GG, SG		
X-Component of Torque			GG, SG		
Y-Component of Torque			GG, SG		
Z-Component of Torque			GG, SG		
Temperature of Solid	GG, SG, VG	GG, SG, VG	GG, SG, VG		PG
Melting Temperature Exceed	SG, VG	SG, VG	SG, VG		PG
Mass Fraction of Air	GG, SG, VG	GG, SG, VG	GG, SG, VG	GG, SG, VG	PG
Volume Fraction of Air	GG, SG, VG	GG, SG, VG	GG, SG, VG	GG, SG, VG	PG
Mass Flow Rate of Air			SG		
Volume Flow Rate of Air			SG		

Table 1.6 List of available parameters for different goals in SolidWorks Flow Simulation

Viewing Results

Results can be visualized in a number of different ways as indicated by table 1.7.

Result Settings								
Results	Cut Plots	3D-Profile Plots	Surface Plots	Isosurfaces	Flow Trajectories	Particle Studies	XY Plots	Point , Surface and Volume Parameters

Table 1.7 List of available results in SolidWorks Flow Simulation

Limitations of SolidWorks Flow Simulation

It is important to know the limitations of SolidWorks Flow Simulation before you start the process of modeling your engineering problem. The limitations include the following common flow situations that can't be studied in the present version of SolidWorks Flow Simulation: chemically reacting flows, free fluid surface flows, fluid mixing flows, multi-phase flows and moving model parts. However, it should be pointed out that motion of walls can be specified as boundary conditions in SolidWorks Flow Simulation. An example of this is shown in chapter 5 where we study Taylor-Couette flow between rotating cylinders.

References

[1] SolidWorks Flow Simulation 2009 Solving Engineering Problems

[2] SolidWorks Flow Simulation 2009 Technical Reference

[3] SolidWorks Flow Simulation 2009 Tutorial

Notes:

Chapter 2   Flat Plate Boundary Layer

Objectives

- Creating the SolidWorks part needed for the Flow Simulation
- Setting up Flow Simulation projects for internal flow
- Setting up a two-dimensional flow condition
- Initializing the mesh
- Selecting boundary conditions
- Inserting global goals, point goals and equation goals for the calculations
- Running the calculations
- Using Cut Plots to visualize the resulting flow field
- Use of XY Plots for velocity profiles, boundary layer thickness, displacement thickness, momentum thickness and friction coefficients
- Use of Excel templates for XY Plots
- Comparison of Flow Simulation results with theories and empirical data
- Cloning of the project

Problem Description

In this chapter, we will use SolidWorks Flow Simulation to study the two-dimensional laminar and turbulent flow on a flat plate and compare with the theoretical Blasius boundary layer solution and empirical results. The inlet velocity for the 1 m long plate is 5 m/s and we will be using air as the fluid for laminar calculations and water to get a higher Reynolds number for turbulent boundary layer calculations. We will determine the velocity profiles and plot the profiles using the well known boundary layer similarity coordinate. The variation of boundary layer thickness, displacement thickness, momentum thickness and the local friction coefficient will also be determined. We will start by creating the part needed for this simulation, see figure 2.0.

Figure 2.0 SolidWorks model for flat plate boundary layer study

Creating the SolidWorks Part

1. Start by creating a new part in SolidWorks: select **File>>New** and click on the **OK** button in the **New SolidWorks Document** window. Click on **Front Plane** in the **FeatureManager design tree** and select **Front** from the **View Orientation** drop down menu in the graphics window.

Figure 2.1a) Selection of front plane

Figure 2.1b) Selection of front view

2. Click on **Corner Rectangle** from the **Sketch** tools.

Figure 2.2a) Selecting a sketch tool

3. Click to the left and below the origin in the graphics window and drag the rectangle to the right and upward. Fill in the parameters for the rectangle: 1000 mm wide and 100 mm high. Close the Rectangle dialog box by clicking on ✓. Right click in the graphics window and select **Zoom/Pan/Rotate>> 🔍 Zoom to Fit**.

Figure 2.3a) Parameter settings for the rectangle

Figure 2.3b) Closing the dialog box

Figure 2.3c) Zooming in the graphics window

4. Repeat steps 2 and 3 but create a larger rectangle outside of the first rectangle. Dimensions are shown in Figure 2.4.

Figure 2.4 Dimensions of second larger rectangle

5. Click on the Features tab and select **Extruded Boss/Base**. Check the box for ☑ **Direction 2** and click ✓ **OK** to exit the **Extrude Property Manager**.

Figure 2.5a) Selection of extrusion feature

Figure 2.5b) Closing the property manager

6. Select **Front** from the **View Orientation** drop down menu in the graphics window. Click on **Front Plane** in the **FeatureManager design tree.** Click on the **Sketch** tab and select the **Line** sketch tool.

Figure 2.6 Selection of the line sketch tool

7. Draw a vertical line in the Y-direction starting at the lower inner surface of the sketch. Set the **Parameters** and **Additional Parameters** to the values shown in the figure. Close the dialog ✓ .

Figure 2.7 Parameters for vertical line

8. Repeat step 7 three more times and add three more vertical lines to the sketch, the second line at X = 400 mm with a length of 40 mm, the third line at X = 600 mm with a length of 60 mm and the fourth line at X = 800 mm with a length of 80 mm. These lines will be used to plot the boundary layer velocity profiles at different streamwise positions along the flat plate. Save the SolidWorks part with the following name: **Flat Plate Boundary Layer Study**. Rename the newly created sketch in the **FeatureManager design tree**, see figure 2.8.

Figure 2.8 Renaming the sketch for boundary layer velocity profiles

9. Repeat step 6 and draw a horizontal line in the X-direction starting at the origin of the lower inner surface of the sketch. Set the **Parameters** and **Additional Parameters** to the values shown in the figure and close the dialog ✅ . Rename the sketch in the **FeatureManager design tree** and call it **x = 0 – 0.9 m**.

Figure 2.9 Adding a line in the X-direction

10. Next, we will create a split line. Repeat step 6 once again but this time select the **Top Plane** and draw a line in the Z-direction through the origin of the lower inner surface of the sketch. It will help to zoom in and rotate the view to complete this step. Set the **Parameters** and **Additional Parameters** to the values shown in the figure and close the dialog ✅ .

Figure 2.10 Drawing a line in the Z-direction

11. Select **Insert>>Curve>>Split Line…** from the SolidWorks menu. For **Faces to Split**, select the surface where you have drawn your split line, see figure 2.11b). Close the dialog ✓ . You have now finished the part for the flat plate boundary layer. Select **File>>Save** from the SolidWorks menu.

Figure 2.11a) Creating a split line

Figure 2.11b) Selection of surface for the split line

Setting Up the Flow Simulation Project

12. If Flow Simulation is not available in the menu, you have to add it from SolidWorks menu: **Tools>>Add Ins…** and check the corresponding **SolidWorks Flow Simulation** box. Select **Flow Simulation>>Project>>Wizard** to create a new Flow Simulation project. Create a new figuration named "**Flat Plate Boundary Layer Study**". Click on the **Next >** button. Select the default **SI (m-kg-s)** unit system and click on the **Next>** button once again.

Figure 2.12a) Starting a new Flow Simulation project

Figure 2.12b) Creating a name for the project

13. Use the default **Internal Analysis type**.

Figure 2.13 Excluding cavities without flow conditions

14. Select **Air** from the **Gases** and add it as **Project Fluid**. Select **Laminar Only** from the **Flow Type** drop down menu. Click on the **Next >** button. Use the default **Wall Conditions** and click on the **Next >** button. Insert **5 m/s** for **Velocity in X-direction** as **Initial Condition** and click on the **Next >** button. Slide the **Result resolution** to **8**. Click on the **Finish** button.

Figure 2.14 Selection of fluid for the project and flow type

15. Select **Flow Simulation>>Computational Domain…**. Click on the **Boundary Condition** tab and select **XY-Plane Flow** from the drop down menu. Click on the **OK** button to exit the **Computational Domain** window.

Figure 2.15a) Modifying the computational domain

Figure 2.15b) Selecting two dimensional flow condition

16. Select **Flow Simulation>>Initial Mesh....** Uncheck the **Automatic setting** box at the bottom of the window. Change both the **Number of cells per X:** to **300** and the **Number of cells per Y:** to **200**. Click on the **OK** button to exit the **Initial Mesh** window.

Figure 2.16a) Modifying the initial mesh

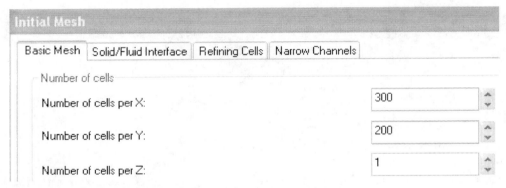

Figure 2.16b) Changing the number of cells in two directions

Selecting Boundary Conditions

17. Select the 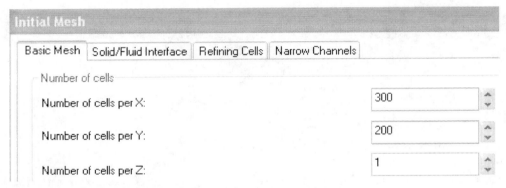 **Flow Simulation analysis tree** tab, open the **Input Data** folder by clicking on the plus sign next to it and right click on **Boundary Conditions**. Select **Insert Boundary Condition....** Right click in the graphics window and select **Zoom/Pan/Rotate>>Rotate View**. Click and drag the mouse so that the inner surface of the left boundary is visible. Right click again and select **Zoom/Pan/Rotate>>Rotate View**. Click on the left inflow boundary surface. Select **Inlet Velocity** in the **Type** portion of the **Boundary Condition** window and set the velocity to **5 m/s** in the **Flow Parameters** window. Click **OK** to exit the window. Right click in the graphics window and select **Zoom/Pan/Rotate>>** **Zoom to Area** and select an area around the left boundary.

Figure 2.17a) Inserting boundary condition   Figure 2.17b) Modifying the view

Figure 2.17c) Including a velocity boundary condition on the inflow

Figure 2.17d) Inlet velocity boundary condition indicated by arrows

18. Red arrows pointing in the right direction appears indicating the inlet velocity boundary condition, see figure 2.17d). Right click in the graphics window and select **Zoom to Fit**. Right click again in the graphics window and select 🔄 **Rotate View** once again to rotate the part so that the inner right surface is visible in the graphics window. Right click and click on ⬉ **Select**. Right click on 📖 **Boundary Conditions** in the **Flow Simulation analysis tree** and select **Insert Boundary Condition….** Click on the end surface on the outlet boundary. Click on the **Pressure Openings** button in the **Type** portion of the **Boundary Condition** window and select **Static Pressure**. If you zoom in on the outlet boundary you will see blue arrows indicating the static pressure boundary condition, see figure 2.18b). Click OK ✔ to exit the window.

Figure 2.18a) Selection of static pressure as boundary condition at the outlet of the flow region

Figure 2.18b) Outlet static pressure boundary condition

19. Enter the following boundary conditions: Ideal Wall for the upper wall and lower wall at the inflow region, see figures 2.19. These will be adiabatic and frictionless walls.

Figure 2.19 Ideal wall boundary condition for upper wall

20. The last boundary condition will be in the form of a real wall. We will study the development of the boundary layer on this wall.

Figure 2.20 Real wall boundary condition for the flat plate

Inserting Global Goals

21. Right click on **Goals** in the **Flow Simulation analysis tree** and select **Insert Global Goals….** Select **X – Component of Shear Force** as a global goal. Exit the **Global Goals** window. Right click on **Goals** in the **Flow Simulation analysis tree** and select **Insert Point Goals….** Click on the $\begin{smallmatrix}x_{Y}\\[-2pt]z\end{smallmatrix}$ **Point Coordinates** button. Enter **0.2 m** for X coordinate and **0.02 m** for Y coordinate and click on the **Add Point** button $\boxed{*^{+}}$. Add three more points with the coordinates shown in figure 2.21e). Check the **Value** box for **X-Component of Velocity**. Exit the **Point Goals** window. Rename the point goals as shown in figure 2.21g). Right click on **Goals** in the **Flow Simulation analysis tree** and select **Insert Equation Goal….** Click on the **X-Component of Velocity at x = 0.2 m** goal in the **Flow Simulation analysis tree**, multiply by 0.2 and divide by the kinematic viscosity of air at room temperature (1.516E-5) to get an expression for the Reynolds number in the **Equation Goal** window, see figure 2.21h). Select **No units** from the dimensionality drop down menu. Rename the equation goal to **Reynolds number at x = 0.2 m**. Insert three more equation goals corresponding to the Reynolds numbers at the three other *X* locations. For a definition of the Reynolds number, see page 2-19.

Figure 2.21a) Inserting global goals

Figure 2.21b) Selection of X – component of shear force

Figure 2.21c) Inserting point goals

Figure 2.21d) Selecting point coordinates

Selection

	X [m]	Y [m]	Z [m]
*	0.2	0.02	0
	0.4	0.02	0
	0.6	0.02	0
	0.8	0.02	0

Figure 2.21e) Coordinates for point goals

Parameter	Value	Use for Conv.
Static Pressure		✓
Total Pressure		✓
Dynamic Pressure		✓
Temperature of Fluid		✓
Density		✓
Velocity		✓
X - Component of Velocity	✓	✓

Figure 2.21f) Parameter for point goals

Figure 2.21g) Renaming the point goals   Figure 2.21h) Entering an equation goal

Running the Calculations

22. Select **Flow Simulation>>Solve>>Run** to start calculations. Click on the **Run** button in the **Run** window. Click on the goals button in the **Solver** window to see the **List of Goals**.

Figure 2.22a) Starting calculations

Figure 2.22b) Run window

Figure 2.22c) Solver window

Using Cut Plots to Visualize the Flow Field

23. Right click on Cut Plots in the **Flow Simulation analysis tree** and select **Insert….** Select the **Front Plane** from the FeatureManager design tree. Click on View Settings…. Slide the **Number of colors:** slide bar to 101. Select **Pressure** from the **Parameter** drop down menu. Click on OK. Click OK to exit the **Cut Plot** window. Figure 2.23a) shows the high pressure region close to the leading edge of the flat plate. Rename the cut plot to **Pressure**. Repeat this step but instead choose **X-velocity** from the **Parameter** drop down menu. Rename the second cut plot to **X-velocity**. Figures 2.23b) and 2.23c) are showing the velocity boundary layer close to the wall.

Figure 2.23a) Pressure distribution along the flat plate.

Figure 2.23b) X-velocity distribution on the flat plate.

Figure 2.23c) Close up view of the velocity boundary layer.

Using XY Plots with Templates

24. Place the file **"xy-plot figure 2.24c)"** into the **Local Disk (C:)/Program Files /SolidWorks (2)/SolidWorks Flow Simulation/lang/english/template/XY-Plots** folder to make it available in the **Template** list. Click on the FeatureManager design tree. Click on the sketch **x = 0.2, 0.4, 0.6, 0.8 m**. Click on the **Flow Simulation analysis tree** tab. Right click **XY Plot** and select **Insert…**. Check the **X-velocity** box. Open the **Resolution** portion of the **XY Plot** window and slide the **Geometry Resolution** as far as it goes to the right. Click on the **Evenly Distribute Output Points** button and increase the number of points to **500**. Open the **Options** portion and check the **Display boundary layer** box. Select the template **"xy-plot figure 2.24c)"** from the drop down menu. Click OK to exit the **XY Plot** window. An Excel file will open with a graph of the velocity in the boundary layer at different streamwise positions, see figure 2.24c). Rename the inserted xy-plot in the Flow Simulation analysis tree to **Laminar Velocity Boundary Layer**.

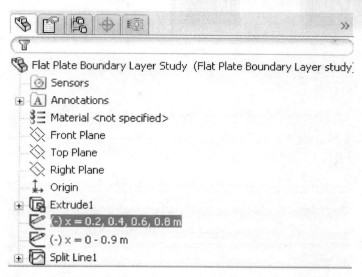

Figure 2.24a) Selecting the sketch for the XY Plot

Figure 2.24b) Settings for the XY Plot

Figure 2.24c) Boundary layer velocity profiles on a flat plate at different streamwise positions

Comparison of Flow Simulation Results with Theory and Empirical Data

25. We now want to compare this velocity profile with the theoretical Blasius velocity profile for laminar flow on a flat plate. First, we have to normalize the steamwise X velocity component with the free stream velocity. Secondly, we have to transform the wall normal coordinate into the similarity coordinate for comparison with the Blasius profile. The similarity coordinate is described by

$$\eta = y\sqrt{\frac{U}{vx}} \qquad (1)$$

where y (m) is the wall normal coordinate, U (m/s) is the free stream velocity, x (m) is the distance from the leading edge and v is the kinematic viscosity of the fluid.

26. Place the file **"xy-plot figure 2.25a)"** into the **Local Disk (C:)/Program Files /SolidWorks (2)/SolidWorks Flow Simulation/lang/english/template/XY-Plots** folder to make it available in the **Template** list. Repeat step 24 and select the new template for the XY-plot. Rename the xy-plot to **Comparison with Blasius Profile**.

We see in figure 2.25a) that all profiles at different streamwise positions approximately collapse on the same Blasius curve when we use the boundary layer similarity coordinate.

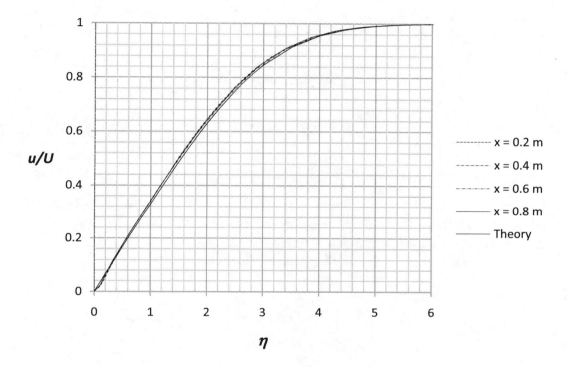

Figure 2.25a) Velocity profiles in comparison with the theoretical Blasius profile (full line)

The Reynolds number for the flow on a flat plate is defined as

$$Re_x = \frac{Ux}{\nu} \tag{2}$$

The boundary layer thickness is defined as the distance from the wall to the location where the velocity in the boundary layer has reached 99% of the free stream value. The theoretical expression for the thickness of the laminar boundary layer is given by

$$\frac{\delta}{x} = \frac{4.91}{\sqrt{Re_x}} \tag{3}$$

and the thickness of the turbulent boundary layer

$$\frac{\delta}{x} = \frac{0.16}{Re_x^{1/7}} \tag{4}$$

From the data of figure 2.24c) we can see that the thickness of the laminar boundary layer is close to 3.88 mm at $Re_x = 66{,}900$ corresponding to $x = 0.2$ m. The free stream velocity at $x = 0.2$ m is $U = 5.069$ m/s, see figure 2.22c) for list of goals in solver window, and 99% of this value is $U_\delta = 5.018$ m/s. The boundary layer thickness from Flow Simulation was found by finding the y position corresponding to the U_δ velocity. This value of the boundary layer thickness can be compared with a value of 3.80 mm from equation (3). In table 2.1 are comparisons shown between boundary layer thickness from Flow Simulation and theory corresponding to the four different Reynolds numbers shown in figure 2.24c). The Reynolds number varies between $Re_x = 66{,}900$ at $x = 0.2$ m and $Re_x = 270{,}900$ at $x = 0.8$ m.

	δ (mm) Simulation	δ (mm) Theory	Percent (%) Difference	U_δ (m/s)	U (m/s)	$\nu\left(\frac{m^2}{s}\right)$	Re_x
$x = 0.2$ m	3.88	3.80	2.4	5.018	5.069	0.00001516	66,900
$x = 0.4$ m	5.41	5.36	1.0	5.044	5.095	0.00001516	134,400
$x = 0.6$ m	6.53	6.55	0.3	5.065	5.116	0.00001516	202,500
$x = 0.8$ m	7.48	7.55	0.9	5.082	5.133	0.00001516	270,900

Table 2.1 Comparison between Flow Simulation and theory for laminar boundary layer thickness

27. Place the file "**xy-plot figure 2.25b)**" into the **Local Disk (C:)/Program Files /SolidWorks (2)/SolidWorks Flow Simulation/lang/english/template/XY-Plots** folder to make it available in the **Template** list. Repeat step 24 and select the new template for the XY-plot as shown in figure 2.25b). Rename the xy-plot to **Boundary Layer Thickness**.

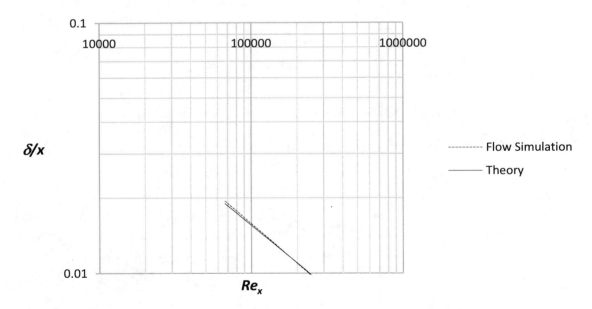

Figure 2.25b) Comparison between Flow Simulation and theory on boundary layer thickness

The displacement thickness is defined as the distance that a streamline outside of the boundary layer is deflected by the boundary layer and is given by the following integral

$$\delta^* = \int_0^\infty (1 - \frac{u}{U})dy \qquad\qquad (5)$$

The theoretical expression for the displacement thickness of the laminar boundary layer is given by

$$\frac{\delta^*}{x} = \frac{1.72}{\sqrt{Re_x}} \qquad\qquad (6)$$

and the displacement thickness of the turbulent boundary layer

$$\frac{\delta^*}{x} = \frac{0.02}{Re_x^{1/7}} \qquad\qquad (7)$$

	δ^* (mm) Simulation	δ^* (mm) Theory	Percent (%) Difference	Re_x
x = 0.2 m	1.3310	1.3303	0.05	66,900
x = 0.4 m	1.8418	1.8766	1.85	134,400
x = 0.6 m	2.2617	2.2936	1.39	202,500
x = 0.8 m	2.5858	2.6439	2.20	270,900

Table 2.2 Comparison between Flow Simulation and theory for laminar displacement thickness

Place the file **"xy-plot figure 2.25c)"** into the **Local Disk (C:)/Program Files /SolidWorks (2)/SolidWorks Flow Simulation/lang/english/template/XY-Plots** folder to make it available in the **Template** list. Repeat step 24 and select the new template for the XY-plot as shown in figure 2.25c). Rename the xy-plot to **Displacement Thickness**.

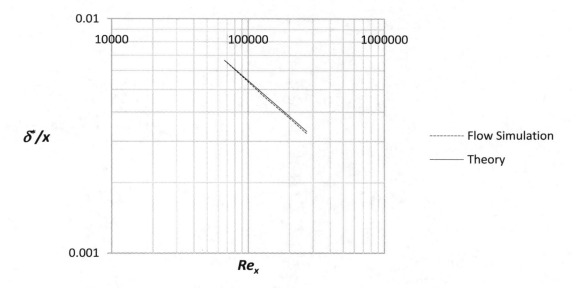

Figure 2.25c) Comparison between Flow Simulation and theory on displacement thickness

The momentum thickness is related to the loss of momentum flux caused by the boundary layer. The momentum thickness is defined by an integral similar to the one for displacement thickness

$$\theta = \int_0^\infty \frac{u}{U}\left(1 - \frac{u}{U}\right)dy \tag{8}$$

The theoretical expression for the momentum thickness of the laminar boundary layer is given by

$$\frac{\theta}{x} = \frac{0.664}{\sqrt{Re_x}} \tag{9}$$

and the momentum thickness of the turbulent boundary layer

$$\frac{\theta}{x} = \frac{0.016}{Re_x^{1/7}} \tag{10}$$

	θ (mm) Simulation	θ (mm) Theory	Percent (%) Difference	Re_x
x = 0.2 m	0.5107	0.5136	0.56	66,900
x = 0.4 m	0.7132	0.7255	1.56	134,400
x = 0.6 m	0.8756	0.8854	1.11	202,500
x = 0.8 m	1.0016	1.0207	1.87	270,900

Table 2.3 Comparison between Flow Simulation and theory for laminar momentum thickness

Place the file **"xy-plot figure 2.25d)"** into the **Local Disk (C:)/Program Files /SolidWorks (2)/SolidWorks Flow Simulation/lang/english/template/XY-Plots** folder to make it available in the **Template** list. Repeat step 24 and select the new template for the XY-plot as shown in figure 2.25d). Rename the xy-plot to **Momentum Thickness**.

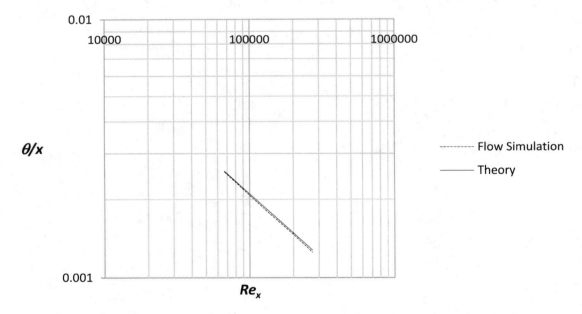

Figure 2.25d) Comparison between Flow Simulation and theory on momentum thickness

Finally, we have the shape factor that is defined as the ratio of the displacement thickness and the momentum thickness.

$$H = \frac{\delta^*}{\theta} \qquad (11)$$

The theoretical value of the shape factor is $H = 2.59$ for the laminar boundary layer and $H = 1.25$ for the turbulent boundary layer.

	H Simulation	H Theory	Percent (%) Difference	Re_x
x = 0.2 m	2.6062	2.59	0.63	66,900
x = 0.4 m	2.5824	2.59	0.29	134,400
x = 0.6 m	2.5830	2.59	0.27	202,500
x = 0.8 m	2.5817	2.59	0.32	270,900

Table 2.4 Comparison between Flow Simulation and theory for laminar shape factor

28. We now want to study how the local friction coefficient varies along the plate. It is defined as the local wall shear stress divided by the dynamic pressure:

$$C_{f,x} = \frac{\tau_w}{\frac{1}{2}\rho U^2} \qquad (12)$$

The theoretical local friction coefficient for laminar flow is given by

$$C_{f,x} = \frac{0.664}{\sqrt{Re_x}} \qquad Re_x < 5 \cdot 10^5 \qquad (13)$$

and for turbulent flow

$$C_{f,x} = \frac{0.027}{Re_x^{1/7}} \qquad 5 \cdot 10^5 \leq Re_x \leq 10^7 \qquad (14)$$

Place the file **"xy-plot figure 2.26"** into the **Local Disk (C:)/Program Files /SolidWorks (2)/SolidWorks Flow Simulation/lang/english/template/XY-Plots** folder to make it available in the **Template** list. Repeat step 24 but this time choose the sketch **x = 0 – 0.9 m**, uncheck the box for **X-Velocity** and check the box for **Shear Stress**. Rename the xy-plot to **Local Friction Coefficient**. An Excel file will open with a graph of the local friction coefficient versus the Reynolds number compared with theoretical values for laminar boundary layer flow.

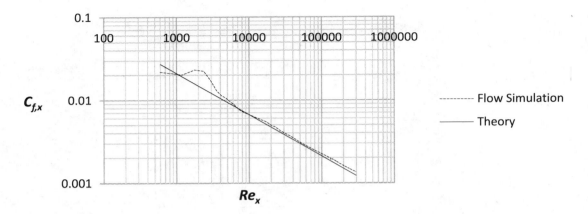

Figure 2.26 Local friction coefficient as a function of the Reynolds number

The average friction coefficient over the whole plate C_f is not a function of the surface roughness for the laminar boundary layer but a function of the Reynolds number based on the length of the plate Re_L, see figure E3 in Exercise 8 at the end of this chapter. This friction coefficient can be determined in Flow Simulation by using the final value of the global goal, the X-component of the Shear Force F_f, see figure 2.22c) and dividing it by the dynamic pressure times the area A in the X-Z plane of the computational domain related to the flat plate.

$$C_f = \frac{F_f}{\frac{1}{2}\rho U^2 A} = \frac{0.000147156 N}{\frac{1}{2} \cdot 1.204 kg/m^3 \cdot 5^2 m^2/s^2 \cdot 1m \cdot 0.004m} = 0.002444 \qquad (15)$$

$$Re_L = \frac{UL}{\nu} = \frac{5m/s \cdot 1m}{1.516 \cdot 10^{-5} m^2/s} = 3.3 \cdot 10^5 \qquad (16)$$

The average friction coefficient from Flow Simulation can be compared with the theoretical value for laminar boundary layers

$$C_f = \frac{1.328}{\sqrt{Re_L}} = 0.002312 \qquad\qquad Re_L < 5 \cdot 10^5 \qquad (17)$$

This is a difference of 5.7 %. For turbulent boundary layers the corresponding expression is

$$C_f = \frac{0.0315}{Re_L^{1/7}} \qquad\qquad 5 \cdot 10^5 \leq Re_L \leq 10^7 \qquad (18)$$

If the boundary layer is laminar on one part of the plate and turbulent on the remaining part the average friction coefficient is determined by

$$C_f = \frac{0.0315}{Re_L^{1/7}} - \frac{1}{Re_L} \left(0.0315 Re_{cr}^{\frac{6}{7}} - 1.328\sqrt{Re_{cr}}\right) \qquad (19)$$

where Re_{cr} is the critical Reynolds number for laminar to turbulent transition.

Cloning of the Project

29. In the next step, we will clone the project. Select **Flow Simulation>>Project>>Clone Project…**. Create a new project with the name "**Flat Plate Boundary Layer Study Using Water**". Click on the OK button to exit the **Clone Project** window. Next, change the fluid to water in order to get higher Reynolds numbers. Start by selecting **Flow Simulation>>General Settings…** from the SolidWorks menu. Click on **Fluids** in the **Navigator** portion and click on the **Remove** button. Select **Water** from the **Liquids** and **Add** it as the **Project Fluid**. Change the **Flow type** to **Laminar and Turbulent**, see figure 2.27d). Click on the OK button to close the **General Setting** window.

Figure 2.27a) Cloning the project

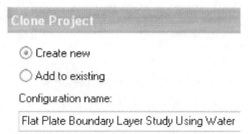

Figure 2.27b) Creating a new project

Figure 2.27c) Selection of general settings

Figure 2.27d) Selection of fluid and flow type

30. Select **Flow Simulation>>Computational Domain...** Set the size of the computational domain to the values shown in figure 2.28a). Click on the OK button to exit. Select **Flow Simulation>>Initial Mesh...** from the SolidWorks menu and change the **Number of cells per X:** to **400** and the **Number of Cells per Y:** to **200**. Also, in the **Control Intervals** portion of the window, change the **Ratio** for **Y1** to **-100** and the **Ratio** for **X1** to **-5**. This is done to increase the number of cells close to the wall where the velocity gradient is high. Click on the OK button to exit. Select **Flow Simulation>>Calculation Control Options...** from the SolidWorks menu. Change the **Maximum travels value** to **5** by first changing to **Manual** from the drop down menu. Travel is a unit characterizing the duration of the calculation. Click on the OK button to exit.

Figure 2.28a) Setting the size of the computational domain

Figure 2.28b) Increasing the number of cells and the distribution of cells

Figure 2.28c) Calculation control options

Figure 2.28d) Setting maximum travels

Select **Flow Simulation>>Project>>Show Basic Mesh** from the SolidWorks menu. We can see in figure 2.28f) that the density of the mesh is much higher close to the flat plate at the bottom wall in the figure as compared to the region further away from the wall.

Figure 2.28e) Showing the basic mesh

Figure 2.28f) Mesh distribution in the X-Y plane

31. Right click the **Inlet Velocity Boundary Condition** in the **Flow Simulation analysis tree** and select **Edit Definition…**. Open the **Boundary Layer** section and select **Laminar Boundary Layer**. Click **OK** ✓ to exit the **Boundary Condition** window. Right click the **Reynolds number at x = 0.2 m** goal and select **Edit Definition…**. Change the viscosity value in the **Expression** to **1.004E-6**. Click on the OK button to exit. Change the other three equation goals in the same way. Select **Flow Simulation>>Solve>>Run** to start calculations. Click on the **Run** button in the **Run** window.

Figure 2.29a) Selecting a laminar boundary layer

Figure 2.29b) Modifying the equation goals

Figure 2.29c) Creation of mesh and starting a new calculation

Figure 2.29d) Solver window and goals table for calculations of turbulent boundary layer

32. Place the file **"xy-plot figure 2.30a)"** into the **Local Disk (C:)/Program Files /SolidWorks (2)/SolidWorks Flow Simulation/lang/english/template/XY-Plots** folder to make it available in the **Template** list. Repeat step 24 and choose the sketch **x = 0.2, 0.4, 0.6, 0.8 m** and check the box for **X-Velocity**. Rename the xy-plot to **Turbulent Velocity Boundary Layer**. An Excel file will open with a graph of the streamwise velocity component versus the wall normal coordinate, see figure 2.30a). We see that the boundary layer thickness is much higher than the corresponding laminar flow case. This is related to higher Reynolds number at the same streamwise positions as in the laminar case. The higher Reynolds numbers are due to the selection of water as the fluid instead of air that has a much higher value of kinematic viscosity than water.

Figure 2.30a) Flow Simulation comparison between turbulent boundary layers at $Re_x = 10^6 - 4.1 \cdot 10^6$

As an example, the turbulent boundary layer thickness from figure 2.30a) is 4.45 mm at $x = 0.2$ m which can be compared with a value of 4.44 mm from equation (4), see table 2.2.

	δ (mm) Simulation	δ (mm) Empirical	Percent (%) Difference	U (m/s)	$\nu\ (\frac{m^2}{s})$	Re_x
x = 0.2 m	4.45	4.44	0.1	5.042	0.000001004	1,004,320
x = 0.4 m	8.73	8.04	8.6	5.070	0.000001004	2,020,100
x = 0.6 m	12.5	11.4	9.9	5.095	0.000001004	3,045,110
x = 0.8 m	16.0	14.5	9.7	5.120	0.000001004	4,079,870

Table 2.5 Comparison between Flow Simulation and empirical results for turbulent boundary layer thickness

Place the file **"xy-plot figure 2.30b)"** into the **Local Disk (C:)/Program Files /SolidWorks (2)/SolidWorks Flow Simulation/lang/english/template/XY-Plots** folder to make it available in the **Template** list. Repeat step 24 and choose the sketch **x = 0.2, 0.4, 0.6, 0.8 m** and check the box for **X-Velocity**. Rename the xy-plot to **Turbulent Boundary Layer Thickness**. An Excel file will open with a graph of the boundary layer thickness versus the Reynolds number, see figure 2.30b).

Figure 2.30b) Boundary layer thickness for turbulent boundary layers at $Re_x = 10^6 - 4.1 \cdot 10^6$

33. Place the file **"xy-plot figure 2.31"** into the **Local Disk (C:)/Program Files /SolidWorks (2)/SolidWorks Flow Simulation/lang/english/template/XY-Plots** folder to make it available in the **Template** list. Repeat step 24 and choose the sketch **x = 0.2, 0.4, 0.6, 0.8 m** and check the box for **X-Velocity**. Rename the xy-plot to **Comparison with One-Sixth Power Law**. An Excel file will open with figure 2.31. In figure 2.31 we compare the results from Flow Simulation with the turbulent profile for $n = 6$. The power –law turbulent profiles suggested by Prandtl are given by

$$\frac{u}{U} = \left(\frac{y}{\delta}\right)^{1/n} \qquad (20)$$

It is seen that for the higher Reynolds numbers in figure 2.31, that the velocity profiles resembles the one-sixth power law.

Figure 2.31 The same profiles as in figure 2.30a) compared with one-sixth power law for turbulent profile.

34. Place the file **"xy-plot figure 2.32"** into the **Local Disk (C:)/Program Files /SolidWorks (2)/SolidWorks Flow Simulation/lang/english/template/XY-Plots** folder to make it available in the **Template** list. Repeat step 24 and choose the sketch **x = 0 – 0.9 m**, uncheck the box for **X-Velocity** and check the box for **Shear Stress**. Rename the xy-plot to **Local Friction Coefficient for Laminar and Turbulent Boundary Layer**. An Excel file will open with figure 2.32. Figure 2.32 is showing the Flow Simulation is able to capture the local friction coefficient in the laminar region in the Reynolds number range 10,000 – 150,000. At Re = 150,000 there is an abrupt increase in the friction coefficient caused by laminar to turbulent transition. In the turbulent

region the friction coefficient is decreasing again but the local friction coefficient from Flow Simulation is significantly higher than empirical data.

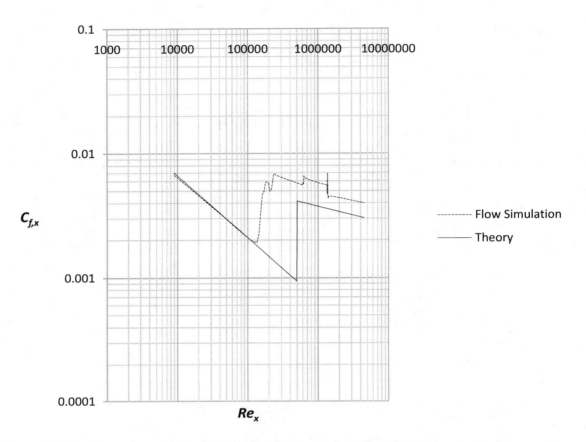

Figure 2.32 A comparison between Flow Simulation (dashed line) and theoretical laminar and empirical turbulent friction coefficients

The average friction coefficient over the whole plate C_f is a function of the surface roughness for the turbulent boundary layer and also a function of the Reynolds number based on the length of the plate Re_L, see figure E3 in Exercise 8. This friction coefficient can be determined in Flow Simulation by using the final value of the global goal, the X-component of the Shear Force F_f and dividing it by the dynamic pressure times the area A in the X-Z plane of the computational domain related to the flat plate, see figure 2.28a) for the size of the computational domain.

$$C_f = \frac{F_f}{\frac{1}{2}\rho U^2 A} = \frac{0.22822N}{\frac{1}{2}\cdot998kg/m^3\cdot5^2m^2/s^2\cdot1m\cdot0.004m} = 0.00457 \tag{21}$$

$$Re_L = \frac{UL}{\nu} = \frac{5m/s\cdot1m}{1.004\cdot10^{-6}m^2/s} = 4.98\cdot10^6 \tag{22}$$

The variation and final values of the goal can be found in the solver window during or after calculation by clicking on the associated flag, see figures 2.33 and 2.29d).

Figure 2.33 Obtaining the current value of the global goal

For comparison with Flow Simulation results we use equation (19) with Re_{cr} = 150,000

$$C_f = \frac{0.0315}{Re_L^{1/7}} - \frac{1}{Re_L} \left(0.0315 Re_{cr}^{\frac{6}{7}} - 1.328\sqrt{Re_{cr}} \right) = 0.0034 \qquad (23)$$

This is a difference of 34%.

References

[1] Çengel, Y. A., and Cimbala J.M., Fluid Mechanics Fundamentals and Applications, 1st Edition, McGraw-Hill, 2006.

[2] Fransson, J. H. M., Leading Edge Design Process Using a Commercial Flow Solver, Experiments in Fluids 37, 929 – 932, 2004.

[3] Schlichting, H., and Gersten, K., Boundary Layer Theory, 8th Revised and Enlarged Edition, Springer, 2001.

[4] SolidWorks Flow Simulation 2009 Technical Reference

[5] White, F. M., Fluid Mechanics, 4th Edition, McGraw-Hill, 1999.

Exercises

1. Change the number of cells per X and Y (see figure 2.16b)) for the laminar boundary layer and plot graphs of the boundary layer thickness, displacement thickness, momentum thickness and local friction coefficient versus Reynolds number for different combinations of cells per X and Y. Compare with theoretical results.

2. Choose one Reynolds number and one value of number of cells per X for the laminar boundary layer and plot the variation in boundary layer thickness, displacement thickness and momentum thickness versus number of cells per Y. Compare with theoretical results.

3. Choose one Reynolds number and one value of number of cells per Y for the laminar boundary layer and plot the variation in boundary layer thickness, displacement thickness and momentum thickness versus number of cells per X. Compare with theoretical results.

4. Import the file "Leading Edge of Flat Plate". Study the air flow around the leading edge at 5 m/s free stream velocity and determine the laminar velocity boundary layer at different locations on the upper side of the leading edge and compare with the Blasius solution. Also, compare the local friction coefficient with figure 2.26. Use different values of the initial mesh to see how it affects the results.

Figure E1. Leading edge of asymmetric flat plate, see Fransson (2004)

5. Modify the geometry of the flow region used in this chapter by changing the slope of the upper ideal wall so that it is not parallel with the lower flat plate. By doing this you get a streamwise pressure gradient in the flow. Use air at 5 m/s and compare your laminar boundary layer velocity profiles for both accelerating and decelerating free stream flow with profiles without a streamwise pressure gradient.

Figure E2. Example of geometry for a decelerating outer free stream flow.

6. Determine the displacement thickness, momentum thickness and shape factor for the turbulent boundary layers in figure 2.30a) and determine the percent differences as compared with empirical data.

7. Change the distribution of cells using different values of the ratios in the X and Y directions, see figure 2.28b), for the turbulent boundary layer and plot graphs of the boundary layer thickness, displacement thickness, momentum thickness and local friction coefficient versus Reynolds number for different combinations of ratios. Compare with theoretical results.

8. Use different fluids, surface roughness, free stream velocities and length of the computational domain to compare the average friction coefficient over the entire flat plate with figure E3.

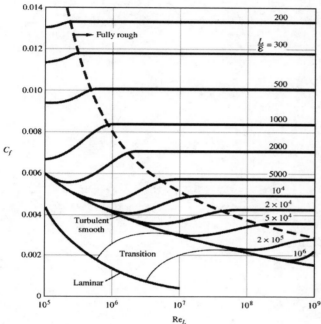

Figure E3 Average friction coefficient for flow over smooth and rough flat plates, White (1999)

Notes:

Chapter 3   Analysis of the Flow past a Sphere and a Cylinder

Objectives

- Creating the sphere and cylinder needed for the SolidWorks Flow Simulation
- Setting up Flow Simulation projects for external flow
- Running the calculations
- Using XY-Plots, Cut Plots and Animation to visualize the resulting flow fields
- Study values of surface parameters
- Cloning of the project
- Run time-dependent calculations to determine the vortex shedding frequency and the Strouhal number for the cylinder
- Compare with empirical results

Problem Description

In this chapter, we will use Flow Simulation to study the three-dimensional flow of air past a sphere with a diameter of 50 mm at different Reynolds numbers and compare with empirical results for the drag coefficient. The second part of this chapter covers the two-dimensional flow around a cylinder and we will determine the Strouhal number related to vortex shedding from the cylinder. We will start by creating the sphere needed for this simulation, see figure 3.0a).

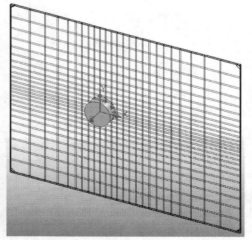

Figure 3.0a) Sphere with 3D mesh   Figure 3.0b) Cylinder with 2D initial mesh

Creating the SolidWorks Part for the Sphere

In this exercise we will analyze the flow around a sphere. First, we have to create a model of the sphere in SolidWorks and export the part to Flow Simulation. Follow these steps to create a solid model of a sphere with 50mm diameter and perform a 3D simulation of the flow field.

1. Start SolidWorks and create a **New Document**.

   The startup window shows **Solidworks Resources** on the right hand side where you can go to the **New Document** icon and select it.

Figure 3.1 SolidWorks startup menu

2. Select **New SolidWorks Document >> Part** and click on the **OK** button.

Figure 3.2 New SolidWorks document selection window

In order to make the sphere we will sketch a half circle in the Front Plane and revolve it. We start this process by making a new sketch.

3. Click on the **Sketch Commands** tab

Figure 3.3 SolidWorks interface

Next, we select the sketch icon in the toolbar to create a new sketch.

4. Click on the **Sketch** icon in the toolbar

Figure 3.4 Creation of a sketch in SolidWorks

In the next window, we have to select the plane where we would like to sketch the half circle of the sphere.

5. Click on the **Front Plane** to select the plane of the sketch.

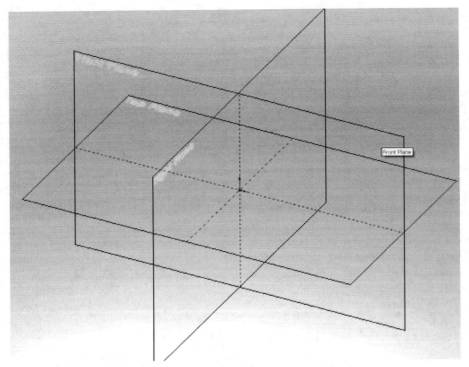

Figure 3.5 Selection of front plane for the sketch

We start sketching by drawing a vertical symmetry line in the sketch plane. This centerline will be used to create the sphere as a revolved feature.

6. Select **Line>>Centerline…**

Figure 3.6 Selection of the centerline sketch tool

7. Next, draw the vertical centerline in the sketch window. Start above the vertical coordinate axis and make sure that you get the blue dashed helpline, see figure 3.7a). Click and draw the line downward through the origin and end the line approximately the same distance below the origin, see figure 3.7b). Right click anywhere in the graphics window and click on **Select**. You have now finished the vertical centerline.

Figure 3.7a) Vertical dashed helpline

Figure 3.7b) Drawing a vertical centerline

Figure 3.7c) Clicking on select

Figure 3.7d) Finished vertical centerline

8. Select the **Centerpoint Arc** from the **Sketch** toolbar and draw the half circle. First, click on the origin, you should see a red filled circle indicating that you are at the origin, see figure 3.8b). Next, click on the centerline above the origin and draw the half circle and click on the centerline once again but this time below the origin. Right click anywhere in the graphics window and click on **Select**.

Figure 3.8a) Selecting centerline arc

Figure 3.8b) Starting at the origin…

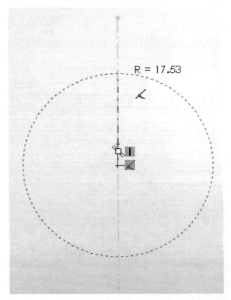

Figure 3.8c) And then above the origin…

Figure 3.8d) Finished half circle

9. Next, select the **Smart Dimension** tool from the **Sketch** toolbar

Figure 3.9 Selecting the Smart Dimension tool

10. Create a radius of 25mm for the half-circle by clicking on the half-circle twice and enter the numerical value in the **Modify** window. Save the value and exit the dialog.

Figure 3.10 Enter a radius of 25mm for the half-circle

The next step is to make the sphere by using the revolve feature in SolidWorks.

11. Click on the **Features Command** tab at the left end of the toolbar. This will insert the **Features** toolbar. Select the **Revolved Boss/Base** icon.

Figure 3.11a) Selection of the Revolved Boss-Base feature

Figure 3.11b) SolidWorks message window

You will get a message that the sketch is currently open and a question if you would like the sketch to be automatically closed. Choose the Yes button.

12. Use the default **Revolve Parameters**: Line 1, One Direction and 360 degrees.
    Click on the OK button with the following green symbol ✔ to exit the **Revolve** window.

Figure 3.12 Selection of default revolve parameters

You have now finished the solid model of the sphere. Complete this part of the exercise by saving the solid model with the name Sphere.

13. Move the cursor to the **File** menu and select **Save As...**
    Enter **Sphere** as File name and click on the **Save** button.

Figure 3.13a) Save the solid model

Figure 3.13b) Finished model

14. Select **Tools>>Add-Ins...**from the menu and check the **SolidWorks Flow Simulation 2009** box.

Add-Ins

Active Add-ins		Start Up
⊟ **SolidWorks Premium Add-ins**		
☐ 3D Instant Website		☐
☐ CircuitWorks		☐
☐ eDrawings 2009		☐
☐ FeatureWorks		☐
☐ PhotoWorks		☐
☐ ScanTo3D		☐
☐ SolidWorks Design Checker		☐
☐ SolidWorks Motion		☐
☐ SolidWorks Routing		☐
☐ SolidWorks Simulation		☐
☐ SolidWorks Toolbox		☐
☐ SolidWorks Toolbox Browser		☐
☐ SolidWorks Utilities		☐
☐ TolAnalyst		☐
⊟ **SolidWorks Add-ins**		
☐ Autotrace		☐
☐ SolidWorks 2D Emulator		☐
☑ SolidWorks Flow Simulation 2009		☐
☐ SolidWorks MTS		☐
☐ SolidWorks XPS Driver		☐

SolidWorks Flow Simulation 2009
SolidWorks Flow Simulation 2009 - Fluid Flow Analysis for SolidWorks

C:\Program Files\SolidWorks (2)
\SolidWorks Flow
Simulation\binCFW\FW03.dll

[OK]   [Cancel]

Figure 3.14 Adding Flow Simulation to the SolidWorks menu

Setting up the Flow Simulation Project for the Sphere

15. We create a project by selecting **Flow Simulation>>Project>>Wizard...** from the menu.

Figure 3.15 Using the Flow Simulation Project Wizard

16. Create a new **Configuration** and enter "**Flow around a Sphere**" as configuration name. Push the **Next>** button.

Figure 3.16 Wizard for the project configuration

17. We choose the **SI (m-kg-s)** unit system and click on the **Next>** button again.

Figure 3.17 Wizard for the unit system

18. Check the **External** option for **Analysis type** and click the **Next>** button

Figure 3.18 General settings of analysis type in Flow Simulation

19. Choose **Air** as the **Default Project Fluid** by clicking on the plus sign next to the **Gases** and selecting **Air**. Next, select the **Add** button. Click on the **Next>** button.

Figure 3.19 Selection of project fluid

The next part of the wizard is about **Wall Conditions**. We will use an **Adiabatic wall** for the sphere and use zero roughness on the surface of the same sphere. Next, we get the **Initial and Ambient Conditions** in the Wizard.

20. Click on the **Next>** button.

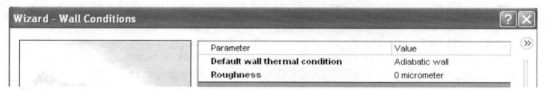

Figure 3.20 Wall conditions wizard

21. Enter **0.003 m/s** as the **Velocity in X-direction** and push the **Next>** button.

Figure 3.21 Initial and ambient conditions wizard

22. Slide the **Result resolution** to **4**. Push the **Finish** button in **Wizard - Results and Geometry Resolution** window. Right click anywhere in the graphics window and select **Zoom In/Out** to see computational domain surrounding the sphere. Select **Flow Simulation>>Project>>Show Basic Mesh** to see the mesh surrounding the sphere, see figure 3.0a).

Figure 3.22a) Result resolution

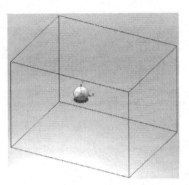

Figure 3.22b) Computational box around the sphere

Inserting Global Goal for Calculations

23. We create global goals for the project by selecting **Flow Simulation>>Insert>>Global Goals...** from the SolidWorks menu and check the box for the **X- Component of Force**. Exit the global goals by clicking on OK ✓. Select **Flow Simulation>>Insert>>Equation Goal...** from the menu and select **GG X-Component of Force 1** from the **Flow Simulation analysis tree**. Enter the expression for the equation goal as shown in figure 3.23e). Select **No units** from the **Dimensionality** drop down menu. Exit the **Equation Goal** window by clicking on the **OK** button. Rename the equation goal in the **Flow Simulation analysis tree** to **Drag Coefficient**.

Figure 3.23a) Selection of global goals

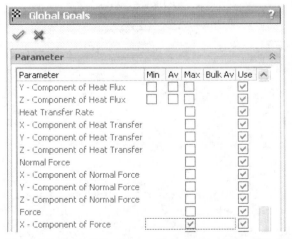

Figure 3.23b) Selection of x- component of force as global goal

Figure 3.23c) Selection of equation goal

Figure 3.23d) Selection of x-component of force for the equation goal

Figure 3.23e) Expression for equation goal

Running the Calculations

Now we are ready to run the simulation. Choose **Flow Simulation>>Solve>>Run...**
Click on the **Run** button in the window that appears. You will get the window shown in figure 3.24a) when you run the calculations.

24. Choose **Flow Simulation>>Solve>>Run...** Click on the **Run** button in the window that appears.

Click on the goals flag to **Insert Goals Table** in the **Solver** window. You will now have the output window shown in figure 3.24a). The CPU time will depend on the speed of your computer and the amount of memory.

Select **Flow Simulation>>Results>>Load/Unload Results**. Repeat this step once again if the **Load Results** window does not open. Select the **Open** button in the **Load Results** window.

Figure 3.24a) Solver window for simulation of the flow around a sphere

Figure 3.24b) Selecting results to load

Figure 3.24c) Loading the results

Using Cut Plots

25. Select the **Flow Simulation analysis tree**

Figure 3.25 Selecting the Flow Simulation analysis tree

For the results section we will start by looking at the velocity distribution around the sphere.

26. Right click on the **Cut Plots** in the **Flow Simulation analysis tree** and select **Insert...** Click on the Vectors button in the **Display** section and push the **View Setting** button. Choose **Velocity** from the **Parameter Settings** drop down menu. Slide **Number of colors** bar to **150**. Click on the **OK** button in the **View Settings** window and exit the **Cut Plots** window. Rename **Cut Plot 1** to **Velocity around Sphere**.

Figure 3.26a) View Settings window in Flow Simulation

We see from the velocity distribution that the maximum velocity is 0.0031184 m/s.

Figure 3.26b) Velocity distribution around the sphere

Inserting Surface Parameters

27. Right-click on **Surface Parameters** in the **Flow Simulation analysis tree** and select **Insert....** Click on the **FeatureManager design tree** and select the **Revolve1** feature. Push the **OK** button in the **Surface Parameters** window. An Excel file is generated with local and integral parameters.

Integral parameters

Parameter	Value	X-component	Y-component	Z-component	Surface area [m^2]
Heat Transfer Rate [W]	0				0.00772809
Normal Force [N]	1.66529E-08	1.66524E-08	8.68449E-11	8.68401E-11	0.00772809
Shear Force [N]	2.68775E-08	2.68774E-08	-4.2378E-11	-5.59376E-11	0.00772809
Force [N]	4.35298E-08	4.35298E-08	4.44669E-11	3.09026E-11	0.00772809
Torque [N*m]	5.71998E-12	-6.84061E-14	4.06596E-12	-4.02262E-12	0.00772809
Surface Area [m^2]	0.00772809	2.96462E-20	1.94818E-19	4.06576E-19	0.00772809
Torque of Normal Force [N*m]	6.78604E-15	5.88009E-16	4.09542E-15	-5.37886E-15	0.00772809
Torque of Shear Force [N*m]	5.7133E-12	-6.89941E-14	4.06187E-12	-4.01724E-12	0.00772809
Uniformity Index [ ]	1				0.00772809
CAD Fluid Area [m^2]	0.00785398				0.00785398

Figure 3.27a) Integral surface parameters

Local parameters

Parameter	Minimum	Maximum	Average	Bulk Average	Surface area [m^2]
Pressure [Pa]	101325	101325	101325		0.00772809
Temperature [K]	293.2	293.2	293.2		0.00772809
Density [kg/m^3]	1.20371	1.20371	1.20371		0.00772809
Velocity [m/s]	0	0	0		0.00772809
X-component of Velocity [m/s]	0	0	0		0.00772809
Y-component of Velocity [m/s]	0	0	0		0.00772809
Z-component of Velocity [m/s]	0	0	0		0.00772809
Mach Number [ ]	0	0	0		0.00772809
Heat Transfer Coefficient [W/m^2/K]	0	0	0		0.00772809
Shear Stress [Pa]	1.19814E-07	7.5772E-06	4.09755E-06		0.00772809
Surface Heat Flux [W/m^2]	0	0	0		0.00772809
Fluid Temperature [K]	293.2	293.2	293.2		0.00772809

Figure 3.27b) Local surface parameters

If we look at the Force related to the Integral parameters we see that the drag force is $D = 4.35298E-08$ N for the X-component. This value can also be found in the **List of Goals** in figure 3.24a).

Theory

The drag coefficient can be determined from the following formula

$$C_D = \frac{D}{\frac{1}{2}\rho U^2 A} = \frac{4.35298\text{E-}08}{\frac{1}{2} \cdot 1.204 \cdot 0.003^2 \cdot \pi \cdot 0.025^2} = 4.092 \qquad (1)$$

, where $\rho\ (kg/m^3)$ is the free-stream density, $U\ (m/s)$ is the free-stream velocity and $A(m^2)$ is the frontal area of the sphere. The Reynolds number is determined by

$$\text{Re} = \frac{Ud\rho}{\mu} = \frac{0.003 \cdot 0.05 \cdot 1.204}{1.825 \cdot 10^{-5}} = 9.9 \qquad (2)$$

where $\mu\ (kg/ms)$ is the dynamic viscosity of air in the free-stream and d is the diameter of the sphere. The drag coefficient can be compared with the following curve-fit from experimental data

$$C_{D,Experiment} = \frac{24}{\text{Re}} + \frac{6}{1+\sqrt{\text{Re}}} + 0.4 = 4.273 \qquad 0 \le \text{Re} \le 200{,}000 \qquad (3)$$

, and we see that the difference in the Flow Simulation result is 4.2 %.

Cloning of the Project

28. We now want to run the computations for different Reynolds numbers. Select **Flow Simulation>>Project>>Clone Project...** from the SolidWorks drop down menu. Create a new project with a different configuration name than the first project, see figure 3.28b). Click on the **OK** button to exit the **Clone Project** window.

Figure 3.28a) Cloning of a project

Figure 3.28b) Entering the name of the cloned project

Time-Dependent Calculations

29. Select **Flow Simulation>>General Settings…** Check the box for Time-dependent flow under **Analysis type** in the **Navigator** for this higher Reynolds number.

Figure 3.29a) Selecting General Settings

Figure 3.29b) Selecting time-dependent flow

30. Select **Initial and ambient conditions** in the **Navigator** and enter the **Velocity in X direction** to **3 m/s**. Click on the **OK** button to exit the **General Settings** window.

Right click on the **Drag Coefficient Goal** in the **Flow Simulation analysis tree** and select **Edit Definition....** Change the velocity in the **Expression** to 3 m/s, see figure 3.30b). Click on the **OK** button to exit the **Equation Goal** window. You are now ready to run the calculations for this higher Reynolds number. Cloning of the project can be repeated and results from a number of runs at different Reynolds numbers will be shown.

Figure 3.30a) Enter velocity in X direction

Figure 3.30b) Expression for equation goal for the higher Reynolds number

31. The following table shows a comparison of the computations and experiments at different Reynolds numbers including the percent difference for the drag coefficient:

U (m/s)	Re	$C_{D,Simulation}$	$C_{D,Experiment}$	Difference (%)
0.00003	0.1	205.0	248	16
0.0003	1.0	25.23	27.7	8.8
0.003	9.9	4.093	4.273	4.2
0.03	99.0	0.8794	1.191	26
0.3	989	0.3682	0.609	40
3.0	9,894	0.2263	0.462	51
30	98,940	0.1829	0.419	56

Table 3.1 Comparison of drag coefficient for a sphere at various Reynolds numbers

Figure 3.31 Comparison of experimental drag coefficient for a sphere and a smooth cylinder. The black circles represents results from Flow Simulation for a sphere.

We see that the Flow Simulation results deviate more and more from experimental results as the Reynolds number is increasing. A finer initial mesh and several levels of refinement is required in order to get results closer to experiments at higher Reynolds numbers. You have now completed your simulation of the flow around a sphere.

Creating the SolidWorks Part for the Cylinder

32. Select **File>>New...** from the SolidWorks menu. Repeat steps 2 – 5 from the beginning of this chapter by selecting a new **Part** and clicking on the **OK** button, see figure 3.32b). Click on the **Sketch Commands** tab and click on the **Sketch** icon in the toolbar. Click on the 🔨 **Front Plane** in the 📦 **FeatureManager design tree** to select the plane of the sketch. Select Front view from the 🔲▾ **View Orientation** drop down menu in the graphics window. Select the **Circle** sketch tool, see figure 3.32e).

Figure 3.32a) Creating a new SolidWorks document

Figure 3.32b) Selection of a new part

Figure 3.32c) Sketch tool

Figure 3.32d) Front view orientation   Figure 3.32e) Circle sketch tool

33. Draw a circle with a radius of **25.00 mm**. Close the **Circle** dialog box. Click on the **Features Command** tab and select the **Extruded Boss/Base** icon. Check the **Direction 2** box and exit the **Extrude** dialog box. Select **File>>Save As** and enter the name "**Cylinder**" as the name for the SolidWorks part.

Figure 3.33a) Sketch of a circle   Figure 3.33b) Selecting extrusion

Setting up the Flow Simulation Project for the Cylinder

34. We create a project by selecting **Flow Simulation>>Project>>Wizard...** from the menu. Create a new **Configuration** and enter "**Flow around a Cylinder**" as configuration name. Push the **Next>** button. We choose the **SI (m-kg-s)** unit system and click on the **Next>** button again.

    In the next step we check **External** as analysis type, check the box for **Time-dependent** flow and then click on the **Next>** button. The **Default Fluid Wizard** will now appear. We are going to add air as the **Project Fluid**. Start by clicking on the plus sign next to the **Gases** in the **Fluids** column. Scroll down the different gases and select air. Next, click on the **Add** button so that air will appear as the **Default Fluid**. Click on the **Next>** button.

    The next part of the wizard is about **Wall Conditions**. We will use an **Adiabatic wall** for the cylinder and use zero surface roughness. Next, we get the **Initial and Ambient Conditions** in the Wizard. We set the **Velocity in X-direction** to **0.06 m/s** and click on the **Next>** button.

    Slide the **Result resolution** to **8**. Push the **Finish** button in **Wizard - Results and Geometry Resolution** window. Right click anywhere in the graphics window and select **Zoom In/Out** to see the computational domain surrounding the cylinder.

Select **Flow Simulation>>Project>>Show Basic Mesh** to see the mesh surrounding the cylinder, see figure 3.0b).

Figure 3.34 Setting for result resolution for cylinder

Inserting Global Goals for Calculations and selecting 2D Flow

35. We create global goals for the project by selecting **Flow Simulation>>Insert>>Global Goals...** from the SolidWorks menu and check the boxes for the **X- Component of Force** and the **Y- Component of Force**. Exit the global goals.

Select **Flow Simulation>>Insert>>Equation Goal...** from the menu and select **GG X- Component of Force 1** from the **Flow Simulation analysis tree**. Enter the expression for the equation goal as shown in figure 3.35a). Select **No units** from the **Dimensionality** drop down menu. Exit the **Equation Goal** window. Rename the equation goal in the Flow Simulation analysis tree to **Drag Coefficient**. Repeat this step and create an equation goal for the lift coefficient, see figure 3.35b).

Select **Flow Simulation>>Computational Domain...** from the SolidWorks menu. Select the **Boundary Condition** tab and **XY-Plane Flow** from the **2D plane flow:** drop down menu, see figure 3.35c). Click on the **OK** button to exit the **Computational Domain** window.

Select **Flow Simulation>>Initial Mesh...** from the SolidWorks menu. Uncheck the **Automatic settings** box at the bottom of the **Initial Mesh** window. Set the **Number of cells per X:** to **25** and the **Number of cells per Y:** to **24**. Click on the **OK** button.

Select **Flow Simulation>>Calculation Control Options...** from the SolidWorks menu. Set **Maximum physical time** to **200 s**. Click on the **OK** button.

Expression:

{GG X - Component of Force 1}*2/(1.204*0.06^2*0.004*0.050)

Figure 3.35a) Expression for equation goal for drag coefficient

Expression:

{GG Y - Component of Force 1}*2/(1.204*0.06^2*0.004*0.050)

Figure 3.35b) Expression for equation goal for lift coefficient

Figure 3.35c) Selecting the computational domain

Tabular Saving

36. We would like to save the calculations at different instants in time so that we can capture the vortex shedding motion. You start by selecting **Flow Simulation>>Calculation Control Options...** from the SolidWorks menu. Select the **Saving** tab and check on the **Value** box next to **Periodic Saving**. Click on the plus sign next to **Periodic Saving** and set the **Start Value** to iteration number **507** and the **Period Value** to **1**, see figure 3.36. Click on the plus sign next to **Tabular Saving**. Select **Physical time (s)** from the **Units** drop down menu and **Click to edit...** the **Saving table**. Click on the **Add Row** button in the **Table** window and add **97.27 s**. Add four more rows with the values as shown in figure 3.36. Click on the **OK** buttons to exit the **Table** and **Calculation Control Options** windows.

Figure 3.36 Calculation control options

Running Calculations for the Cylinder

37. Choose **Flow Simulation>>Solve>>Run...** Click on the **Run** button in the window that appears. Click on the goals flag ▨ to **Insert Goals Table** in the **Solver** window. Click on ☒ **Insert Goals Plot** in the **Solver** window. Select **Lift Coefficient** as goal. Click on the **OK** button. Right click in the goals plot. Select **Physical time** from **X-axis units**. Slide the **Plot length** to the middle in between **min** and **max**, see figure 3.37a). Click on the **OK** button.

Figure 3.37a) Settings for goal plot

Figure 3.37b) Plot of lift coefficient variation over time

Using Excel for Frequency Analysis

38. We are now interested in determining the frequency of the time signal in figure 3.37b). In order to use FFT (Fast Fourier Transform) calculations in Excel 2007 we have to add the analysis tool packages. Click on the Office button and select [Excel Options]. Click on [Add-Ins] button in the Excel Options window. Select [Excel Add-ins ▼] from the Manage: drop down menu and click on the [Go...] button. Check the boxes for **Analysis ToolPak** and **Analysis ToolPak – VBA**. Click on the OK button. You will now install the add-ins. Place the file **"goals for FFT"** into the **Local Disk (C:)/Program Files /SolidWorks (2)/SolidWorks Flow Simulation/lang/english/template/Goals** folder to make it available in the goals **Template** list.

Figure 3.38a) Using Excel 2007 to add analysis   Figure 3.38b) Adding analysis tools

Inserting XY Plots

39. Right click and select **Insert...** on 🏁 **Goals** in the 📊 **Results** section of the 🔷 **Flow Simulation analysis tree**. Check the box for **Lift Coefficient**, see figure 3.39a). Select **Physical time** from the **Abscissa** drop down menu. Select **goals for FFT.xlt** from the **Template:** drop down menu. Click on the **OK** button. An Excel file will open with the lift coefficient time series plot and another plot for the amplitude versus frequency of the power spectrum from the FFT analysis of the time signal, see figures 3.39b) and 3.39c). We see that the amplitude and period of the time signal is constant in the region from 70s – 200s, compare with 3.37b). The spectrum in figure 3.39c) is a result of using Fourier analysis on this time signal. We see that there is a clear peak in amplitude at a frequency between 0.2 Hz and 0.4 Hz. A more exact value of the frequency can be found from plot data to be 0.238 Hz.

Figure 3.39a) Setting for goals plot

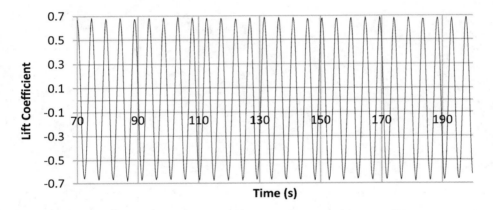

Figure 3.39b) Time signal of the lift coefficient in the region T = 70 – 200 s

Figure 3.39c) Waveform in the frequency domain

Strouhal number

The Strouhal number S is one of the many non-dimensional numbers used in fluid mechanics and based on the oscillation frequency of fluid flows. In this case the Strouhal number is based the vortex shedding frequency f and can be defined as

$$S = \frac{fD}{U} = \frac{0.238 \text{ Hz} \cdot 0.050m}{0.06m/s} = 0.198 \tag{4}$$

The Reynolds number for the flow around a cylinder that we have been studying is

$$\text{Re} = \frac{Ud\rho}{\mu} = \frac{0.06 \cdot 0.050 \cdot 1.204}{1.825 \cdot 10^{-5}} = 198 \tag{5}$$

This value of the Strouhal number from Flow Simulation can be compared with DNS (Direct Numerical Simulations) results of Henderson (1997), see also Williamson and Brown (1998).

$$S = 0.2698 - \frac{1.0272}{\sqrt{\text{Re}}} = 0.1968 \tag{6}$$

The difference is only 0.8%.

Inserting Cut Plots

40. We now want to plot the X-velocity component, pressure and vorticity at the different instants that we tabulated in step 36.

Figure 3.40a) Viewing settings and loading results

Time = 97.27 s, Iteration = 507, Lift Coefficient = 0

Time = 98.44 s, Iteration = 517, Lift Coefficient = 0.685

Time = 99.65 s, Iteration = 527, Lift Coefficient = 0

Time = 100.8 s, Iteration = 536, Lift Coefficient = -0.67

Time = 102 s, Iteration = 546, Lift Coefficient = 0

Figure 3.40b) X-velocity and pressure during a period of vortex shedding

T = 97.27 s, Cl = 0

T = 98.44 s, Cl = 0.685

T = 99.65 s, Cl = 0

T = 100.8 s, Cl = -0.67

T = 102 s, Cl = 0

Figure 3.40c) Vorticity during a period of vortex shedding

Select **Flow Simulation>>Results>>View Settings…** from the SolidWorks menu, see figure 3.40a). Click on the **Parameter List** button in the **View Settings** window. Select the **Scalar Parameters** tab and click on the plus sign next to **Local**. Enable the local parameter named **Vorticity**. Select the **Vector Parameters** tab and click on the plus sign next to **Local**. Enable the local parameter named **Vorticity**. Click on the **OK** buttons to exit the **Display Parameters** and **View Settings** windows.

Select **Flow Simulation>>Results>>Load Time Moment…** from the SolidWorks menu, see figure 3.40a). Open the file **r_000507 .fld**. The number **507** is the iteration number corresponding to calculation time **97.27 s**. Right click on **Cut Plots** in the **Flow Simulation analysis tree** and select **Insert…**. Click on the **View Settings…** button and select **X-velocity** from the **Parameter** drop down menu. Set the **Number of colors** to **254**. Click on the OK button to exit the view settings window and exit the cut plot dialog. Select front view from the view orientation drop down menu in the graphics window. Change the name of Cut Plot 1 to **X-velocity at T = 97.27 s**. Insert two more cut plots and plot the pressure and vorticity, respectively. Click on the **Reset Min/Max** button in the **View Settings** window for each new vorticity cut plot that you create. Change the names of the cut plots to **Pressure at T = 97.27 s** and **Vorticity at T = 97.27 s**. Load the remaining four files **r_000517.fld**, **r_000527.fld**, **r_000536.fld** and **r_000546 .fld**. Plot X-velocity, pressure and vorticity for each file, see figures3.40b) and 3.40c).

Animating the Cut Plots

41. We now want to animate the cut plots of vorticity. Start by selecting **Flow Simulation>>Results>>Load/Unload Results**. Repeat this step one more time if the **Load Result** window does not appear the first time. Click on the **Open** button in the **Load Result** window.

Right click on the cut plot named **Vorticity at T = 97.27 s** and select **Animate…**. Click on **More…** to expand the animation controls section, see figure 3.41a). Click on the control point for **Animation 1** at 00:10 and drag it towards 00:00, see figure 3.41b). Select the animation wizard, see figure 3.41c). Set the animation time to **4.4723 s** and click on the **Next>** button. Click on the **Next>** button in following window. Check the **Scenario** animation type click on the **Next>** button. **Start from: 97.27 s** and **Finish at 102.258 s**, see figure 3.41d). Click on the **Finish** button to exit the animation wizard. Click on the right control point for vorticity located close to 0 s and drag it to 4.6 s, see figure 3.41e). Click on the **Settings** tab and set the frame rate to 50 frames per second. Click on the ▷ **Play** button to start the animation.

Figure 3.41a) Animation controls

Figure 3.41b) Moving of an animation control point

Figure 3.41c) Animation wizard

Figure 3.41d) Setting of time interval for animation

Figure 3.41e) Moving the right control point for vorticity

Figure 3.41f) Setting the frame rate for the animation

References

[1] Çengel, Y. A., and Cimbala, J.M., Fluid Mechanics: Fundamentals and Applications, McGraw-Hill, 2006.

[2] Henderson, R., Nonlinear dynamics and pattern formation in turbulent wake transition, *J. of Fluid Mech.*, **352**, (65-112), 1997.

[3] SolidWorks Flow Simulation 2009 Technical Reference

[4] SolidWorks Flow Simulation 2009 Tutorial

[5] White, F. M., Viscous Fluid Flow, McGraw-Hill, 1991.

[6] Williamson, C. H. K., and Brown G.L., A series in $1/\sqrt{Re}$ to represent the Strouhal-Reynolds number relationship of the cylinder wake, *Journal of Fluids and Structures*, **12**, (1073 – 1085), 1998.

Exercises

1. Run the calculations for the flow over a 25 mm radius sphere for Re = 10, 100 and use different levels of initial mesh: 3, 4 and 5. Plot the drag coefficient versus mesh level and study the percent difference variation as compared with the experimental values $C_{D,Sphere-Experiment}$ = 4.242 and 1.185, respectively. Use the following size of the computational domain: Xmin: -0.175, Xmax: 0.275, Ymin: -0.175, Ymax: 0.175, Zmin: -0.175, Zmax: 0.175.

2. Run the calculations for the flow around a 25 mm radius sphere for Re = 10 for an initial mesh level of 4 and use different sizes of the computational domain:

a) Xmin: -0.05, Xmax: 0.05, Ymin: -0.05, Ymax: 0.05, Zmin: -0.05, Zmax: 0.05
b) Xmin: -0.1, Xmax: 0.1, Ymin: -0.1, Ymax: 0.1, Zmin: -0.1, Zmax: 0.1
c) Xmin: -0.15, Xmax: 0.15, Ymin: -0.15, Ymax: 0.15, Zmin: -0.15, Zmax: 0.15

How does the drag coefficient vary with the size of the computational domain?

3. Use SolidWorks Flow Simulation to determine the drag coefficient for a cylinder with a radius of 25 mm and a length of 350 mm. Use 2D-plane, XY-plane flow boundary condition for the calculations at Re = 0.1, 1, 10, 100, 1000, 10000, 100000 (initial mesh level of 6) and compare with experimental results from Fig. 3.31 and the following curve-fit formula:

$$C_{D,Cylinder-Experiment} = 1 + \frac{10}{Re^{2/3}} \qquad 0 \le Re \le 250,000$$

Determine the percentage difference from experiments in a table for the different Reynolds numbers.

Notes:

Chapter 4   Analysis of the Flow past an Airfoil

Objectives

- Creating the wing section needed for the SolidWorks Flow Simulation
- Inserting a curve through given coordinates
- Setting up a Flow Simulation project for external flow
- Inserting global goals and equation goal
- Running the calculations
- Using Cut Plots to visualize the resulting flow field
- Creating a custom visualization parameter
- Cloning of the project
- Create a batch run
- Compare with experimental results

Problem Description

In this exercise we will analyze the flow around a Selig/Donovan SD 2030 airfoil section. We will study the flow at a Reynolds number $Re = 100,000$ and determine the lift coefficient versus the angle of attack and compare with experimental data. First, we have to create a model of the airfoil in SolidWorks and export the part to Flow Simulation. The chord length of the airfoil is 305 mm and the thickness is 26.1 mm. Follow the different steps in this chapter to create a solid model of the airfoil, see figure 4.0 and perform a 2D plane Flow Simulation of the flow field.

Figure 4.0 SolidWorks model of Selig/Donovan SD 2030 airfoil section

Creating the SolidWorks Part

1. Start SolidWorks and create a New Part. Select the **Front** view from the drop down menu in the graphics window.

Figure 4.1 Selection of front view

2. Select **Insert>>Curve>>Curve Through XYZ Points…**

Figure 4.2 Importing coordinates for the SD 2030 profile

3. In the **Curve File** window you select **Browse** and open the file **SD2030.sldcrv**. The Curve File window appears again with the X and Y coordinates shown for the airfoil. Click **OK**. Right click in the graphics window and **Zoom/Pan/Rotate>>Zoom In/Out**.

Figure 4.3 Imported curve in the form of an airfoil

4. Next, we select the **Front Plane** in the **FeatureManager design tree**, select the **Features** tab and click on the **Extruded Boss/Base** feature.

Figure 4.4 Selection of front plane and extruded boss/base feature

5. Click on **Curve1** in the **FeatureManager design tree**, click on the **Sketch** tab and select the **Convert Entities** tool.

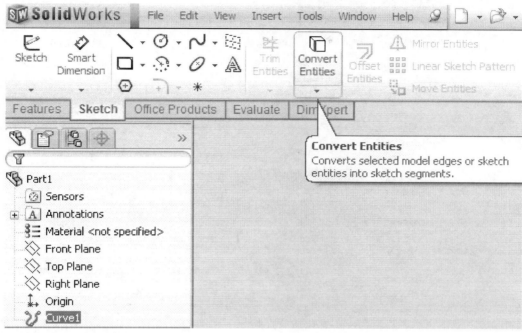

Figure 4.5 Converting entities

6. Select the **Features** tab and **Extruded Boss/Base** once again.

Figure 4.6 Extruding the airfoil sketch

7. Check the box for **Direction 2** and click on the **OK** ✓ button.

Figure 4.7 Entering the direction of the extrusion

8. Select the **Front** view from the drop down menu in the graphics window.
Right click in the graphics window and select **Zoom/Pan/Rotate>>Zoom to Fit**. Save your airfoil as SD 2030.

Figure 4.8 Selecting zoom to fit

9. Click on the plus sign next to the **Extrude1** symbol in the **FeatureManager design tree** and rename the sketch to **Airfoil Sketch** and the extrusion to **Extruded Airfoil Sketch**. You have now finished your SD 2030 section.

Figure 4.9 Rename the extrusion

Setting up the Flow Simulation Project

10. If Flow Simulation is not available in the SolidWorks menu, select **Tools>>Add Ins...** and check the corresponding **SolidWorks Flow Simulation** box. We will now create a Flow Simulation project by selecting **Flow Simulation>>Project>>Wizard...** from the menu. Create a new configuration in the **Project Configuration** window and enter **2D Flow around SD 2030 Airfoil** as the configuration name. Click on the **Next>** button

Figure 4.10 Project configuration wizard

11. Chose **SI Unit system** and click on the **Next>** button

Figure 4.11 Unit system wizard

12. Check the **External Analysis type** box and click the **Next>** button.

Figure 4.12 Analysis type

13. Choose **Air** from the gases in the **Fluids** window and push the **Add** button. Air will now appear as the **Default Project Fluid**. Click on the **Next>** button.

Figure 4.13 Default fluid wizard

14. In the next step we will leave the default value of the surface roughness as **Wall Condition** and click on the **Next>** button. Enter **4.9 m/s** as the **Velocity in X direction** and **0.12%** as **Turbulence intensity** from the **Turbulence Parameters** section. Click on the **Next>** button. Slide the **Result resolution** to **6** in the **Results and Geometry Resolution** window and push the **Finish** button.

Figure 4.14 Adding velocity and turbulence intensity

15. Select **Flow Simulation>>Computational Domain…** from the menu.

Figure 4.15 Selecting the computational domain in Flow Simulation

16. Select the **Boundary Condition** tab and **XY-Plane Flow** from the **2D plane flow** drop down menu. Click on the Size tab and set the Size of the computational domain as shown in figure 4.16b). Click on the **OK** button to close the **Computational Domain** window.

Select **Flow Simulation>>Calculation Control Options…** from the SolidWorks menu. Select the **Finish** tab and **Finish Conditions**. Select **Manual** from the drop down menu of **Value** for **Maximum travels**. Set the value to **5**. Click on the **OK** button to close the **Calculation Control Options** window.

Figure 4.16a) Selecting 2D plane flow

Figure 4.16b) Setting the size of the computational domain

Figure 4.16c) Selecting calculation control options

Figure 4.16d) Selecting the value for maximum travel

Inserting Global Goals for Calculations

17. Click on the **Flow Simulation analysis tree** tab and open the **Input Data** folder by clicking on the plus sign next to it. Right click on **Goals** and select **Insert Global Goals…**. Check the box for **Y-Component of Force** and click on the **OK** button to exit the **Global Goals** window.

Figure 4.17 Selecting global goal

18. Right click in the graphics window and select **Zoom In/Out** and zoom out until you can see the whole computational domain around the airfoil. Select **Flow Simulation>>Project>>Show Basic Mesh** to display the mesh around the airfoil.

Figure 4.18a) Displaying the mesh around the airfoil

Figure 4.18b) Mesh around the airfoil

Running the Calculations

19. Select **Flow Simulation>>Solve>>Run**. Push the **Run** button in the Run window.

Figure 4.19 Starting the calculations of the flow field

20. Click on **Insert Goals Table** to show the goal in the solver window. The following **Solver** window appears as the calculations are running.

Figure 4.20 Solver window for simulation of the flow around an airfoil

Using Cut Plots

21. Select the **Flow Simulation** tab connected to the **Flow Simulation analysis tree**

Figure 4.21 Selecting the Flow Simulation analysis tree

22. Hide the mesh around the airfoil. Right-click on the **Cut Plots** in the **Flow Simulation analysis tree** and select **Insert...** Click on the **View Settings...** button, set the **Number of colors:** to **254** and exit both the view settings and the cut plot windows. Select **Flow Simulation>>Results>>Display>>Lighting**. Rename the **Cut Plot** to in the **Flow Simulation analysis tree** to **Pressure**.

Figure 4.22 Pressure distribution around a SD 2030 airfoil.

23. Right-click on **Surface Parameters** in the **Flow Simulation analysis tree** and select **Insert....** Click on the **FeatureManager design tree** and select the **Extruded Airfoil Sketch**. Push the **OK** button in the **Surface Parameters** window. An Excel file is generated with local and integral parameters.

Integral parameters

Parameter	Value	X-component	Y-component	Z-component	Surface area [m^2]
Heat Transfer Rate [W]	0				0.00246359
Normal Force [N]	0.00101117	0.000129364	0.00100287	0	0.00246359
Shear Force [N]	0.000143692	0.000143535	6.70474E-06	-1.39064E-22	0.00246359
Force [N]	0.0010458	0.000272899	0.00100957	-1.39064E-22	0.00246359
Torque [N*m]	0.00024598	1.76589E-11	-7.01077E-11	0.00024598	0.00246359
Surface Area [m^2]	0.00246359	1.99053E-20	-1.62387E-18	0	0.00246359
Torque of Normal Force [N*m]	0.000246457	8.43724E-23	6.74669E-24	0.000246457	0.00246359
Torque of Shear Force [N*m]	4.76815E-07	1.76589E-11	-7.01077E-11	-4.76815E-07	0.00246359
Uniformity Index [ ]	1				0.00246359
CAD Fluid Area [m^2]	0.00247582				0.00247582

Figure 4.23 Integral Surface Parameters

Theory

If we look at the Force related to the Integral parameters we see that the lift force is $L = 0.00100957$ N for the Y-component and the drag force is $D = 0.000272899$ N for the X-component. The lift and drag coefficients can be determined from

$$C_L = \frac{L}{\frac{1}{2}\rho U^2 bc} = \frac{0.00100957}{\frac{1}{2}\cdot 1.204 \cdot 4.9^2 \cdot 0.004 \cdot 0.305} = 0.0573 \tag{1}$$

$$C_D = \frac{D}{\frac{1}{2}\rho U^2 bc} = \frac{0.000272899}{\frac{1}{2}\cdot 1.204 \cdot 4.9^2 \cdot 0.004 \cdot 0.305} = 0.0155 \tag{2}$$

where $\rho \ (kg/m^3)$ is the free-stream density, $U \ (m/s)$ is the free-stream velocity, $b \ (m)$ is the airfoil wing span, and $c(m)$ is the chord length of the airfoil. The value for b used is the difference between Z max and Z min in the computational domain.

The lift coefficient has been determined using Flow Simulation at zero angle of attack and at a Reynolds number determined by

$$\text{Re} = \frac{Uc\rho}{\mu} = \frac{4.9 \cdot 0.305 \cdot 1.204}{1.8 \cdot 10^{-5}} = 100{,}000 \tag{3}$$

, where $\mu \ (kg/ms)$ is the dynamic viscosity of air in the free-stream.

Next, we want to plot the pressure distribution on the airfoil expressed in dimensionless form by the pressure coefficient

$$C_p = \frac{p_i - p}{\frac{1}{2}\rho U^2} \tag{4}$$

, where $p_i \ (Pa)$ is the surface pressure at location i and $p \ (Pa)$ is the pressure in the free-stream.

Creating a Custom Visualization Parameter

24. Select **Flow Simulation>>Tools>>Engineering Database...** from the menu

Figure 4.24 Selecting the Engineering Database

25. In the **Database tree** expand the **Custom Visualization Parameters** item, right-click the **User Defined** item and select **New Item**.

Figure 4.25 Creating a New Visualization Parameter

26. Under the **Item properties** tab type the parameter's **Name** to **Pressure Coefficient**

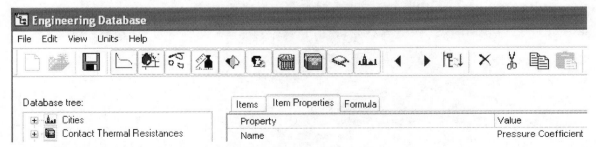

Figure 4.26 Enter a name for the new parameter

27. In the **Formula** row click in on **...** and specify the parameter definition through the **Visualization parameters** drop down menu where you select **Pressure.** The formula that you enter will be the following: ({Pressure}-101324)/(0.5*1.204*4.9^2). Select **File, Save** from the **Engineering Database** menu and exit the engineering database window.

Figure 4.27 Entering a formula for the new parameter

28. Select **Flow Simulation>>Results>>Parameter List...** from the menu

Figure 4.28 Select the parameter list from the results in Flow Simulation

29. Check the **Enabled** box for the **Pressure Coefficient Parameter.** Click on the **OK** button.

Figure 4.29 Enabling the Pressure Coefficient parameter

30. Right-click on the **XY Plots** and select **Insert…** from the **Flow Simulation analysis tree**. Click on the **FeatureManager design tree** tab and select the **Airfoil Sketch** under the **Extruded Airfoil Sketch**. Next, check **Pressure Coefficient** in the **Parameter** list of the **XY Plot window** and choose **Sketch X** for the **Abscissa** in the same window. Open the **Options** portion of the **XY Plot** window and select the template **xy-plots.xlt** from the drop down menu.

Figure 4.30 XY plot window settings

31. Click on the green **OK** ✓ button and an Excel graph will be generated showing the variation of the pressure coefficient over the airfoil. Rename the **XY Plot** in the **Flow Simulation analysis tree** to **Pressure Coefficient**.

Figure 4.31 Variation of pressure coefficient on SD 2030 airfoil

32. Insert a new **Cut Plot** in the **Flow Simulation analysis tree**, push the **View Setting** button in the window that appears. Choose **Velocity** from the **Parameter Settings** drop down menu. Click **OK** in the **View Settings** window and click on the OK buttons to display the velocity field over the airfoil. Rename the **Cut Plot** to **Velocity**.

Figure 4.32 Velocity field around a SD 2030 airfoil

Inserting Equation Goal for Calculations

33. Right-click on **Goals** under **Input Data** in the **Flow Simulation analysis tree** and select **Insert Equation Goal…**. Enter the expression for the lift coefficient by clicking on the **GG Y – Component of Force 1** goal under **Goals** in the **Flow Simulation analysis tree**. Complete the expression as shown in figure 4.33b). Select **No units** from the **Dimensionality:** drop down menu. Click **OK** to exit the **Equation Goal** window. Rename the equation goal to **Lift Coefficient** in the **Flow Simulation analysis tree**.

Figure 4.33a) Inserting an equation goal

Figure 4.33b) Entering the expression for the lift coefficient

Cloning of the Project

34. Select **Flow Simulation>>Project>>Clone Project….** Create a cloned project with the name "**2D Flow around SD 2030 Airfoil at 2 deg. Angle of Attack**". Click on the **OK** button to exit the **Clone Project** window.

Figure 4.34 Cloning of the project

35. Select **Flow Simulation>>General Settings.** Click on **Initial and ambient conditions** in the **Navigator**. Enter **4.897 m/s** as **Velocity in X-direction** and **0.171 m/s** as **Velocity in Y-direction** corresponding to an angle of attack of 2°. Click on the **OK** button to exit the window. Repeat steps 34 and 35 four more times and change the angles of attack and corresponding velocity components as shown in table 4.1.

Figure 4.35 Selection of general settings

Angle of Attack	X – Velocity (m/s)	Y – Velocity (m/s)
0°	4.9000	0.0000
2°	4.8970	0.1710
4°	4.8881	0.3418
6°	4.8732	0.5122
8°	4.8523	0.6819
10°	4.8256	0.8509

Table 4.1 Velocity component for different angles of attack

Creating a Batch Run

36. Select **Flow Simulation>>Solve>>Batch Run...**. Make sure to check all boxes as shown in figure 4.36b). Click on the **Run** button to start the calculations.

Figure 4.36a) Starting the batch run for different angles of attack

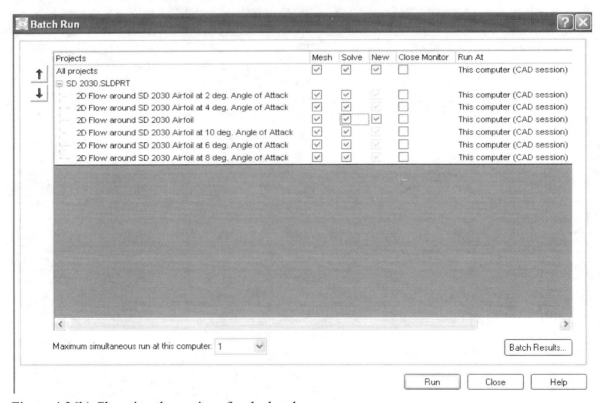

Figure 4.36b) Changing the settings for the batch run.

Angle of Attack Simulation	Lift Coefficient Simulation	Angle of Attack Experiment	Lift Coefficient Experiment
0°	0.0573	0.11	0.122
2°	0.2707	1.14	0.231
4°	0.4841	2.17	0.403
6°	0.5814	3.17	0.574
8°	0.7209	4.26	0.693
10°	0.7734	5.29	0.784
		6.32	0.873
		7.33	0.945
		8.34	1
		9.36	1.051
		10.34	1.09
		11.39	1.105

Table 4.2 Lift coefficient for different angles of attack, experimental results from Selig and McGranaham (2004)

The figure below shows a comparison of experimental results and Flow Simulation calculations for Re = 100,000. It is seen that the Flow Simulation values for the lift coefficient are lower than the corresponding values from experiments.

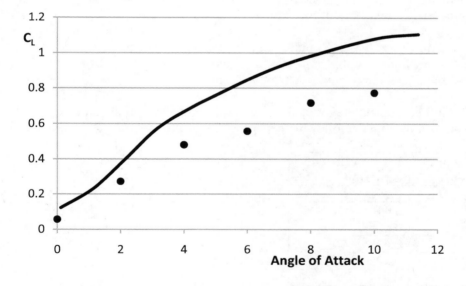

Figure 4.36c) Comparison of experiments (line) with Flow Simulation results (circles)

Reference

[1] Selig M.S. and McGranaham B., Wind Tunnel Aerodynamics Tests of Six Airfoils for Use on Small Wind Turbines, NREL/SR-500-34515, National Renewable Energy Laboratory, May 2004.

Exercises

1. Run the calculations for the flow over a SD 2030 airfoil for Re = 200,000 and use different levels of initial mesh. Plot the lift coefficient versus mesh level and study the percent difference variation as compared with the experimental values

Angle of Attack	Lift Coefficient
0.15	0.252
1.17	0.391
2.23	0.499
3.21	0.593
4.22	0.690
5.26	0.784
6.30	0.869
7.34	0.945
8.35	1.012
9.34	1.070
10.37	1.112
11.38	1.138

Table E1 Experimental values of lift coefficient for SD 2030 and Re = 200,000, from Selig and McGranaham (2004)

2. Run the calculations for the flow over a SD 2030 airfoil for Re = 500,000 for an initial mesh level of 6 and use different sizes of the computational domain:

    a) Xmin: -0.2 m, Xmax: 0.4 m, Ymin: -0.2 m, Ymax: 0.2 m
    b) Xmin: -0.4 m, Xmax: 0.6 m, Ymin: -0.4 m, Ymax: 0.4 m
    c) Xmin: -1 m, Xmax: 2 m, Ymin: -1 m, Ymax: 1 m

How does the lift coefficient vary with the size of the computational domain?
Compare your results with the following experimental results as shown in table E2.

Angle of Attack Experiment	Lift Coefficient Experiment
0.20	0.291
1.16	0.410
2.23	0.525
3.24	0.628
4.28	0.725
5.28	0.814
6.30	0.909
7.34	0.993
8.36	1.012
9.34	1.068
10.42	1.176
11.4	1.199

Table E2 Experimental values of lift coefficient for SD 2030 and Re = 500,000, from Selig and McGranaham (2004)

Chapter 5   Rayleigh-Bénard Convection and Taylor-Couette Flow

Objectives

- Creating the SolidWorks models needed for Flow Simulations
- Setting up Flow Simulation projects for internal flows
- Creating lids for boundary conditions and setting up boundary conditions
- Use of gravity as a physical feature and running the calculations
- Using cut plots and surface plots to visualize the resulting flow field
- Compare results with linear stability theory

Problem Description

In this chapter we will study roll cell instabilities in two simple geometries. We will start by looking closer at the flow caused by natural convection between a hot bottom wall and an upper colder wall, see figure 5.0a). This flow case is known as Rayleigh-Bénard convection. We will use water as the fluid and only a very small temperature difference is required to get the primary instability in this flow. The lower hot wall will be set to 295 K and the upper cold wall to 293 K. The depth of the fluid layer is 4.793 mm and the inner diameter of the enclosure is 100 mm. The second flow case that will be studied in this chapter is Taylor-Couette flow, see figure 5.0b), the flow between two vertical and rotating cylinders. In this chapter, we will rotate the inner cylinder at 5 rad/s and keep the outer cylinder stationary. The inner and outer cylinders have radii of 30 mm and 35 mm, respectively and the height of the cylinders is 100 mm. A centrifugal instability will cause the appearance of counter-rotating vortices at low rotation speed of the inner cylinder. For both flow cases, comparisons will be made with linear stability theory.

Figure 5.0a) Model of Rayleigh-Bénard convection cell   Figure 5.0b) Taylor-Couette cell

Creating the SolidWorks Part for Rayleigh-Bénard Convection

1. Start SolidWorks and create a New Part. Select the **Front** view from the **View Orientation** drop down menu in the graphics window and click on the **Front Plane** in the **FeatureManager design tree**. Next, click on the **Sketch Command** tab and select the **Circle** sketch tool.

Figure 5.1a) Front Plane

Figure 5.1b) Selection of the **Circle** sketch tool

2. Click on the origin in the graphics window and create a circle. Enter 50 mm for the radius of the circle in the **Parameters** box. Close the dialog box.

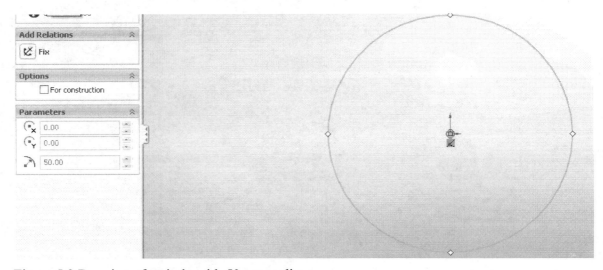

Figure 5.2 Drawing of a circle with 50 mm radius

3. Draw another larger circle concentric with the first circle and enter 55 mm for the radius. Close the dialog box.

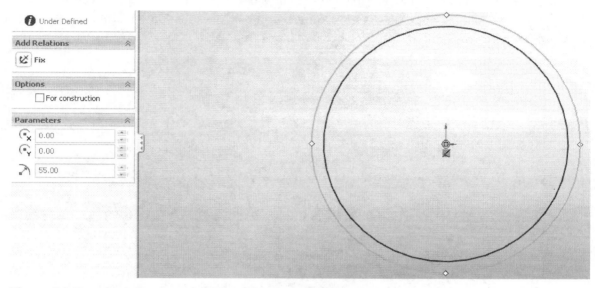

Figure 5.3 Drawing of a second circle with 55 mm radius

4. Next, make and extrusion by selecting **Extruded Boss/Base** from the **Features** tab. Enter 3.175mm in **Direction 1** and the same depth in **Direction 2**. Close the dialog box. Save the part with the name **Rayleigh-Benard Cell**.

Figure 5.4a) Entering depth   Figure 5.4b) Extruded ring

Setting up the Flow Simulation Project for Rayleigh-Bénard Convection

5. If Flow Simulation is not available in the SolidWorks menu, select **Tools>>Add Ins...** and check the corresponding **SolidWorks Flow Simulation** box. Start the **Flow Simulation Wizard** by selecting **Flow Simulation>>Project>>Wizard** from the SolidWorks menu.

Figure 5.5 Starting the Flow Simulation Project Wizard

6. Create a new configuration with the following name: **Convection in Rayleigh-Benard Cell**.

Figure 5.6 Entering configuration name

7. Select the SI unit system

Figure 5.7 Selection of unit system

8. Select the default **Internal Analysis type** and enter **-9.81 m/s^2** as **Gravity** for the **Z component** in **Physical Features**.

Figure 5.8 Enter gravity as physical feature

9. Add **Water** as the default **Project Fluid** by selecting it from **Liquids**. Choose default values for **Wall Conditions, Initial Conditions** and **Results and Geometry Resolution**.

Figure 5.9 Adding the default fluid

Creating Lids

10. Next, we have to add a lid on both sides of the ring to create an enclosure. Click on one of the two plane surfaces of the ring and select **Flow Simulation>>Tools>>Create Lids**. Note that the thickness of the lid is close to 0.7785 mm. This means that the final thickness of the fluid layer will be 4.793 mm. Click ✔ **OK** and answer yes to the question whether you want to reset the mesh setting that appears in the graphics window.

Figure 5.10 Selecting the surface

11. Next, right click in the graphics window and select **Rotate View**. Rotate the ring with a lid around. Select the other plane surface of the ring and create the second lid with the same thickness as the first lid. Answer "Yes" when asked to reset the computational domain and mesh settings. Select **Hidden Lines Visible** from the **Display Style** drop down menu in the graphics window.

Figure 5.11a) Selection of 2nd surface   Figure 5.11b) Making hidden lines visible

Inserting Boundary Conditions for Rayleigh-Bénard Convection

12. Click on the **Flow Simulation analysis tree** tab and click on the plus sign next to the **Input Data** folder. Right click on **Boundary Conditions** and select **Insert Boundary Condition…**

Figure 5.12 Selecting boundary conditions.

13. Right click in the graphics window and select **Zoom/Pan/Rotate>>Rotate View**. Rotate the enclosure so that it has the same view as in figure 5.13a), right click and click on **Rotate View**. Move the cursor over the top lid, right-click again and click on **Select Other**. Select the face for the inner upper surface of the enclosure. Select the **Wall** button and select **Real Wall** boundary condition. Set the value of **293 K** for the wall temperature in the **Wall Parameters** window. Click ✔ **OK** to finish the first boundary condition. Rename the boundary condition from **Real Wall 1** to **Top Wall**.

Figure 5.13a) View of enclosure for upper boundary condition

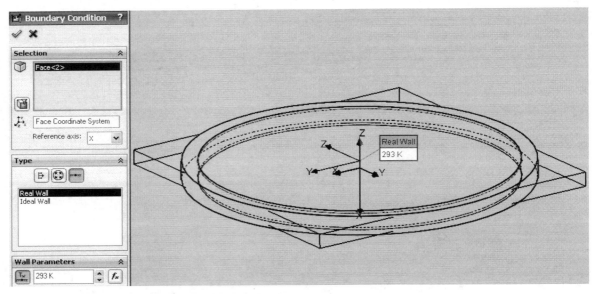

Figure 5.13b) Selection of boundary condition for upper surface

14. Repeat steps 12 and 13 but select the inner lower surface and enter **295 K** as wall temperature. Rename the boundary condition from **Real Wall 2** to **Bottom Wall**.

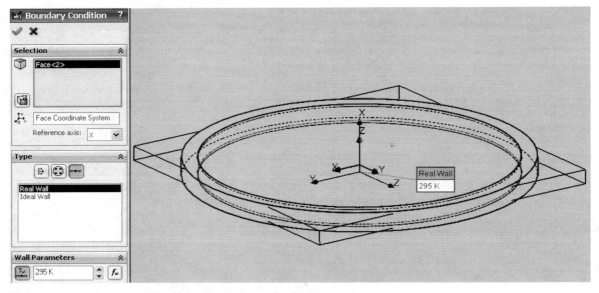

Figure 5.14 Selection of boundary condition for lower surface

15. Repeat steps 12 and 13 and select the remaining inner cylindrical surface and enter **293 K** as wall temperature. Rename the boundary condition from **Real Wall 3** to **Side Wall**.

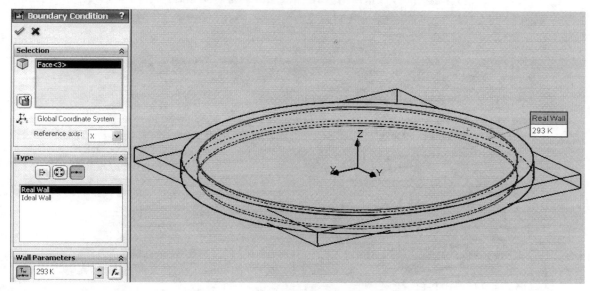

Figure 5.15 Selection of boundary condition for cylindrical surface

Setting up 2D Flow

16. Choose **Flow Simulation>>Computational Domain…**. Click on the **Boundary Condition** tab and select **XZ-Plane Flow**. Click on the **OK** button.

Figure 5.16a) Modifying the computational domain

Figure 5.16b) Selecting XZ-Plane Flow

Inserting Global Goal for Rayleigh-Bénard Convection

17. Right click on **Goals** in the **Flow Simulation analysis tree** and select **Insert Global Goals…** Check the boxes for **Min, Av** and **Max Temperature of Fluid** and **Min, Av** and **Max Z – Component of Velocity**.

Figure 5.17a) Inserting global goals   Figure 5.17b) Temperature and velocity as goals

Running the Calculations

18. Select **Flow Simulation>>Solve>>Run**. Push the **Run** button in the window that appears.

Figure 5.18 Starting the calculation of temperature and flow fields

19. Insert the goals table by clicking on the flag in the **Solver** as shown in figure 5.19a).

Figure 5.19a) Inserting goals

Figure 5.19b) Solver window

Inserting Cut Plots

20. Right click on **Cut Plots** in the **Flow Simulation analysis tree** and select **Insert...**. Select the **Top Plane** from the **FeatureManager design tree** and click on **View Setting...** .Slide the **Number of colors:** setting to **101**. Select **Temperature** from the **Parameters** drop down menu and push the **Reset Min/Max** button followed by the **OK** button. Click ✔ **OK** one again to exit the **Cut Plot**. Rename **Cut Plot 1** and name it **Temperature**.

Figure 5.20a) Selection of top plane for cut plot

Figure 5.20b) Settings for cut plot

21. Click on **Section View** in the graphics window. Select the **Top Plane** in the **Section 1** window.

Click ✔ **OK** to exit the **Section View**. Right click on the **Computational Domain** located in the **Input Data** folder of the **Flow Simulation analysis tree** and select **Hide**. The color bar showing the temperature scale is hidden at the left side of the graphics window but can be moved closer to the cut plot. In figure 5.21c) is the temperature field shown with the hot bottom wall and the colder upper wall. Plumes of hot water are seen rising from the hot wall.

Figure 5.21a) Creating a section view

Figure 5.21b) Selection of top plane

Figure 5.21c) Temperature field in Rayleigh-Bénard cell

22. Repeat step 20 but select **Z-velocity** from the **Parameters** drop down menu in the **View Settings** window. Also, click on the ⬚ **Vectors** button in the **Cut Plot** settings. Next, select the **Flow Simulation** tab and click on **Lighting** to display the Z-velocity field in figure 5.22b). Alternating regions of positive and negative z-velocity indicate the presence of counter-rotating vortices in the cell. The counter-rotating motion of the vortices is shown by the vectors.

Figure 5.22a) Adding some light to the cut plot

Figure 5.22b) Z-velocity field in Rayleigh-Bénard cell

Comparison with Neutral Stability Theory

23. The instability of the flow between two parallel plates heated from below is governed by the so called Rayleigh number Ra.

$$Ra = \frac{g\beta(T_1-T_2)L_c^3}{v^2} Pr \tag{1}$$

where g is acceleration due to gravity, β is the coefficient of volume expansion, T_1 and T_2 are the temperatures of the hot and cold surfaces respectively, L_c is the distance between the surfaces. Pr is the Prandtl number and v is the kinematic viscosity of the fluid. Below the critical $Ra_{crit} = 1708$ for a rigid upper surface, the flow is stable but convective currents will develop above this Rayleigh number. For the case of a free upper surface, the theory predicts a lower critical Rayleigh number. Unfortunately, Flow Simulation is not able to model free surface boundary conditions. The non-dimensional wave number α of this instability is determined by

$$\alpha = \frac{2\pi L_c}{\lambda} \tag{2}$$

where λ is the wave length of the instability. The critical wave numbers are $\alpha_{crit} = 3.12, 2.68$ for rigid and free surface boundary conditions, respectively. From figure 5.22b) the wave number can be determined to be

$$\alpha = \frac{2\pi \cdot 0.004793}{0.00909} = 3.31 \tag{3}$$

The Rayleigh number in the Flow Simulation is

$$Ra = \frac{9.81*0.000195*2*0.004793^\wedge 3}{10^\wedge(-12)} * 7.01 = 2953 \tag{4}$$

The neutral stability curve can be given to the first approximation, see figure 5.23.

$$Ra = \frac{(\pi^2+\alpha^2)^3}{\alpha^2\left\{1-16\alpha\pi^2 cosh^2(\frac{\alpha}{2})/[(\pi^2+\alpha^2)^2(sinh\alpha+\alpha)]\right\}} \tag{5}$$

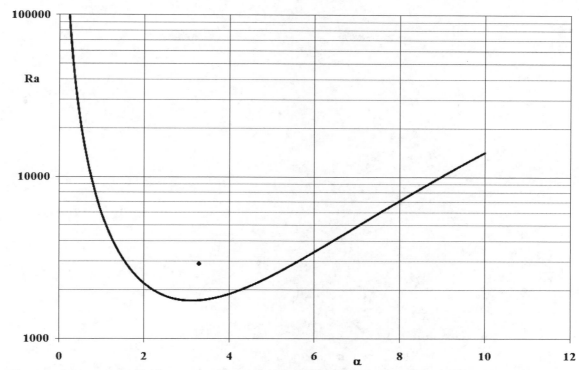

Figure 5.23 Neutral stability curve for Rayleigh-Bénard convection. The filled circle represents result from Flow Simulation.

Creating the SolidWorks Part for Taylor-Couette Flow

The second flow case that we will run in this chapter is Taylor-Couette flow, the flow between rotating cylinders. In this case, we will have an inner rotating cylinder and a stationary outer cylinder. We start by creating the part using SolidWorks.

24. Start by repeating steps 1 – 3 from the beginning of this chapter. Start SolidWorks and create a New Part. Select the **Front** view from the **View Orientation** drop down menu in the graphics window and click on the **Front Plane** in the **FeatureManager design tree**. Next, click on the **Sketch Command** tab and select the **Circle** sketch tool. Click on the origin in the graphics window and create a circle. Enter **25 mm** for the radius of the circle in the **Parameters** box. Close the dialog box. Draw another larger circle concentric with the first circle and enter **30 mm** for the radius. Close the dialog box.

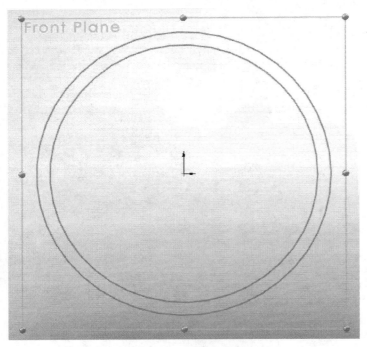

Figure 5.24 Two circles for the inner cylinder

25. The two circles for the outer cylinder are drawn in the next step. The radii for these two circles are **35 mm** and **40 mm**.

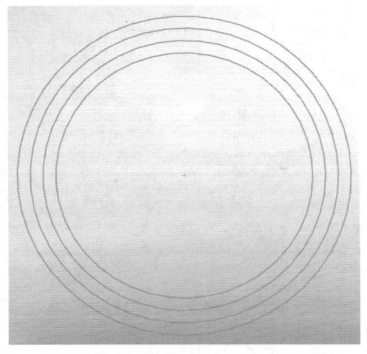

Figure 5.25 Adding two more circles for the outer cylinder.

26. Click on **Sketch 1** in the **FeatureManager design tree** followed by the selection of **Extruded Boss/Base** from the **Features** tab. Select the two sketch regions for extrusion and enter a depth of 50 mm in both **Direction 1** and **Direction 2**. Click on OK ✓ . Save the part with the name **Taylor-Couette Cell**.

Figure 5.26a) Selection of Sketch 1 for extrusion.   Figure 5.26b) Entering depth of extrusion

 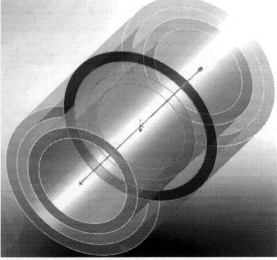

Figure 5.26c) Inner sketch region   Figure 5.26d) Outer sketch region

Setting up the Flow Simulation Project for Taylor-Couette Flow

27. If Flow Simulation is not available in the SolidWorks menu, select **Tools>>Add Ins...** and check the corresponding **SolidWorks Flow Simulation** box. Start the Flow Simulation Wizard by selecting **Flow Simulation>>Project>>Wizard**. Create a new configuration with the following name: **Instabilities in Taylor-Couette flow**.

Figure 5.27 Create a new configuration name

28. Select the **SI unit system** in the next step followed by selection of the default **Internal Analysis type**. Add **Water** as the **Project Fluid** and use default values of wall conditions, initial conditions and set the initial mesh to **5** in the results and geometry resolution window. Next, we create lids by selecting **Flow Simulation>>Tools>>Create Lids...**. Select the outer ring as the face for the lid and click OK ✔. Answer yes to the question whether you want to reset the mesh setting. Next, right click in the graphics window and select **Rotate View**. Rotate the Taylor-Couette model around. Select the outer ring and create the second lid. Answer "**Yes**" when asked to reset the computational domain and mesh settings.

Select **Flow Simulation>>Initial Mesh** from the SolidWorks menu. Uncheck the box for **Automatic settings**. Set the number of cells in all three directions X, Y and Z to **30**. Click on the **OK** button to exit the **Initial Mesh** window. Select **Flow Simulation>>Calculation Control Options...** from the SolidWorks menu. Click on the **Refinement** tab and select **level = 1** for the **Value** of the **Refinement Parameter**. Click on the **OK** button to exit the **Calculation Control Options** window.

Figure 5.28a) Selection of lids for the Taylor-Couette cell

Figure 5.28b) Selection of a lid for the Taylor-Couette cell

29. Select **Hidden Lines Visible** from the **Display Type** drop down menu in the graphics window and **Isometric** view from the **View Orientation** drop down menu.

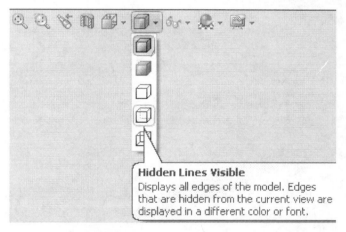

Figure 5.29a) Showing hidden lines

Figure 5.29 Selection of isometric view

Inserting Boundary Conditions for Taylor-Couette Cell

30. Click on the **Flow Simulation analysis tree** tab and click on the plus sign next to the **Input Data** folder. Right click on **Boundary Conditions** and select **Insert Boundary Condition...** Move the cursor over the top lid, right click and select **Select Other**. Select the face for the inner cylindrical surface of the flow domain, see figures 5.30 and 5.0b). Select the **Real Wall** boundary condition, check the box for **Wall Motion** and set the value of **1.5 rad/s** for the angular velocity in the **Z direction** in the **Wall Motion** window, see figure 5.30. Click OK ✅ to finish the boundary condition. Rename the boundary condition in the Flow Simulation analysis tree to **Inner Cylinder**. Insert another boundary condition for the outer cylinder wall, select the **Real Wall** boundary condition without wall motion and name the boundary condition **Outer Cylinder**. Finally, include two more boundary conditions, one for the top wall and another for the bottom wall, both real walls without wall motion and name them **Top Wall** and **Bottom Wall**, respectively, see also figure 5.0b) for position of the different cylinders and walls.

Figure 5.30 Selection of boundary condition for rotating inner cylinder.

Inserting Global Goal and Running the Calculations for Taylor-Couette Flow

31. Right click on **Goals** in the **Flow Simulation analysis tree** and select **Insert Global Goals...**

    Check the boxes for **Min**, **Av** and **Max Velocity** and exit ✓ the window. Select **Flow Simulation>>Solve>>Run**. Push the **Run** button in the window that appears.

Figure 5.31a) Selecting velocity as global goal

Figure 5.31b) Solver window for calculations of Taylor-Couette flow

Inserting Surface Plots

32. Right click on **Surface Plots** in the **Flow Simulation analysis tree** and select **Insert...** Select the face of the rotating cylinder by moving the cursor over the cylinders followed by a right click and **Select Other**. Select the face corresponding to the rotating inner cylinder. Expand **Options** and check the **Offset** box. Click on **View Settings...** and select **Z-Velocity** from the **Parameter:** drop down menu. Slide the number of colors to **254**, close the window and click **OK** ✓ .

Figure 5.32 Surface plot settings.

33. Select **Section View** from graphics window and select **Top Plane** as **Reference Section Plane/Face**. Next, select the **Flow Simulation** tab and click on **Lighting**. The velocity field is shown in figure 5.33d). Alternating bands of high and low velocity are shown in the spanwise Z direction indicating the presence of Taylor vortices. It should be remembered that the surface plot is not on the rotating cylinder but offset in the radial direction towards the outer cylinder. In figures 5.33d), 5.33e) and 5.33f) are two cut plots also added, one in the top plane and another in the front plane.

Select **Flow Simulation>>Results>>View Settings** from the SolidWorks menu. Click on the **Parameter List...** button, select the **Scalar Parameters** tab and enable the following two **Local Parameters**: **Circumferential Velocity** and **Radial Velocity**. Click on the **OK** button to exit the **Display Parameters** window. Click on the **OK** button to exit the **View Settings** window.

Furthermore, in figure 5.33f), the **Reset Plot Min** and **Max** buttons have been used in the **View Settings** window to display a broader spectrum of different colors.

Figure 5.33a) Selection of section view

Figure 5.33b) Selection of top plane

Figure 5.33c) Adding light to the surface plot

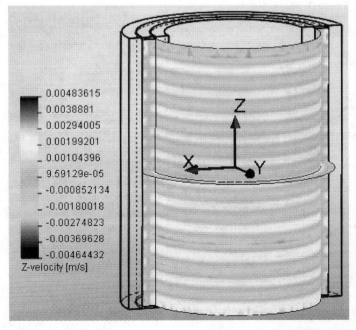

Figure 5.33d) Surface plot and two cut plots for Taylor-Couette flow: Z-velocity

Figure 5.33e) Surface plot and two cut plots for Taylor-Couette flow: Circumferential Velocity

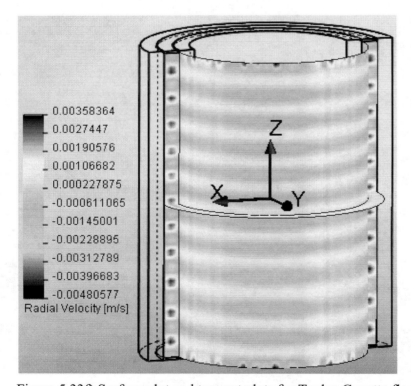

Figure 5.33f) Surface plot and two cut plots for Taylor-Couette flow: Radial Velocity

Comparison with Neutral Stability Theory

34. The instability of the flow between two vertical rotating cylinders is governed by the so called Taylor number Ta.

$$Ta = \frac{4\Omega_i^2 d^4}{\nu^2} \tag{6}$$

where Ω_i is the rotation rate of the inner cylinder, d is the distance between the cylinders and ν is the kinematic viscosity of the fluid. Below the critical $Ta_{crit} = 3412$ for a non-rotating outer cylinder, the flow is stable but instabilities will develop above this Taylor number. The non-dimensional wave number α of this instability is determined by

$$\alpha = \frac{2\pi d}{\lambda} \tag{7}$$

where λ is the wave length of the instability. The critical wave numbers are $\alpha_{crit} = 3.12$ in the narrow gap limit: $\eta \to 1$. The radius ratio is defined as $\eta = r_i/r_o$ where r_i and r_o is the radius of the inner and outer cylinder, respectively. From figures 5.33e), the wave number can be determined to be

$$\alpha = \frac{2\pi \cdot 0.005}{0.00894} = 3.51 \tag{8}$$

The Taylor number in the calculations is

$$Ta = \frac{4 \cdot 1.5^2 \cdot 0.005^4}{(1.004 \cdot 10^{-6})^2} = 5580 \tag{9}$$

The neutral stability curve can be given to the first approximation by, see figure 5.34.

$$Ta = \frac{2(\pi^2+\alpha^2)^3}{(1+\mu)\alpha^2\left\{1-16\alpha\pi^2\cosh^2(\frac{\alpha}{2})/[(\pi^2+\alpha^2)^2(\sinh\alpha+\alpha)]\right\}} \tag{10}$$

where $\mu = \Omega_o/\Omega_i$ and Ω_o is the rotation rate of the outer cylinder.

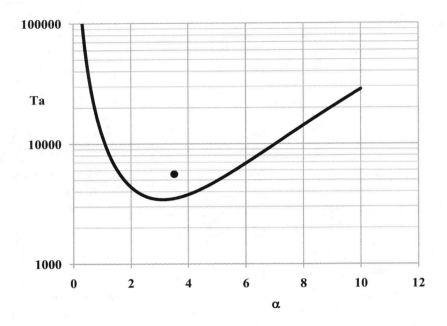

Figure 5.34 Neutral stability curve for Taylor-Couette flow with a stationary outer cylinder, $\mu = 0$. The filled circle represents result from Flow Simulation. The radius ratio $\eta = 6/7$ in the Flow Simulation calculations and $\eta = 1$ for the stability curve.

References

[1] Chandrasekhar, S., Hydrodynamic and Hydromagnetic Stability, Dover, 1981.

[2] Koschmieder, E.L., Bénard Cells and Taylor Vortices, Cambridge, 1993.

Exercises

1. Run the calculations for the flow in the Taylor-Couette apparatus with only the inner cylinder rotating $\mu = 0$ for Taylor numbers $Ta = 10000$, 20000 and 30000 and compare the spanwise wave numbers with the one determined in this chapter for $Ta = 5580$. Include your results in figure 5.34 for comparison with the neutral stability curve.

2. Run the calculations for the flow in the Taylor-Couette apparatus with both cylinders rotating $\mu = 1$ and for Taylor numbers $Ta = 3000$, 5000 and 10000 and determine the spanwise wave numbers. Include your results in a graph and compare with the neutral stability curve corresponding to $\mu = 1$, see equation 10.

3. Run the calculations for the flow in a Rayleigh-Bénard cell for Rayleigh numbers $Ra = 5000$, 10000 and 20000 and compare the wave numbers with the one determined in this chapter for $Ra = 2953$. Include your results in figure 5.23 for comparison with the neutral stability curve.

Chapter 6   Pipe Flow

Objectives

- Creating the SolidWorks model of the pipe needed
- Setting up Flow Simulation projects for internal flows
- Creating a fluid with a certain value of dynamic viscosity
- Creating lids for boundary conditions
- Setting up boundary conditions
- Running the calculations
- Using cut plots and XY plots to visualize the resulting flow field
- Compare results with theory and empirical data

Problem Description

In this chapter, we will use Flow Simulation to study flows in pipes and compare with the theoretical solutions and empirical data. First, we will model the laminar flow with a mean velocity of 0.5 m/s corresponding to a Reynolds number $Re = 100$ for a 5 m long pipe with an inner diameter of 200 mm. Next, we will consider turbulent flow in the same pipe extended to a length of 10 m and a higher Reynolds number $Re = 100,000$. We start by creating the part needed for this simulation.

Figure 6.0 SolidWorks model of pipe section

Creating the SolidWorks Part

1. Start by creating a new part in SolidWorks: select **File>>New** and click on the **OK** button in the **New SolidWorks Document** window. Click on **Right Plane** in the **FeatureManager design tree** and select **Right** from the **View Orientation** drop down menu in the graphics window.

Figure 6.1a) Selection of right plane   Figure 6.1b) Selection of right view

2. Click on **Circle** from the **Sketch** tools tab.

Figure 6.2 Selecting a sketch tool

3. Click on the origin in the graphics window and create a circle. Fill in the **Parameters** for the circle: **100 mm** radius. Close the **Circle** dialog box by clicking on ✔ . Repeat this step and create another concentric circle with a larger radius of **120 mm**.

Figure 6.3 Two concentric circles with radii 100 mm and 120 mm

4. Click on the **Features** tab and select **Extruded Boss/Base**. Enter a **Depth D1** of **5000 mm** in **Direction 1**. Next, click ✔ **OK** to exit the **Extrude Property Manager**.

Figure 6.4a) Selection of extrusion feature

Figure 6.4b) Entering depth for extrusion

5. Select **Wireframe** from the **Display Style** drop down menu in the graphics window. Select **Front** from the **View Orientation** drop down menu in the graphics window. Click on **Front Plane** in the **FeatureManager design tree.** Right click in the graphics window and select **Zoom/Pan/Rotate>>Zoom to Area** and zoom in around the left end of the pipe.

Figure 6.5a) Displaying
the wireframe style

Figure 6.5b) Selection of zoom to area tool

6. Click on the **Sketch** tab and select the **Line** sketch tool. Draw a vertical line in the Y-direction starting at the origin in the center of the pipe and end at the inner surface of the pipe. Right click in the graphics window and click on **Select**. Click on the new line and set the **Parameters** and **Additional Parameters** to the values shown in the figure. Close the ⬛ **Line Properties** dialog ✓ .

Figure 6.6a) Selection of the line sketch tool

Figure 6.6b) Parameters for vertical line

7. Repeat step **6** and draw five more vertical lines with the same length, the lines positioned at x = 200, 400, 600, 800 and 4600 mm. These lines will be used to plot the velocity profiles at different streamwise positions along the pipe. Rename the newly created sketch in the **FeatureManager design tree** and name it **x = 0, D, 2D, 3D, 4D, 23D**, see figure 6.7b).

Figure 6.7a) Sketch lines along the pipe for velocity profiles

Figure 6.7b) Renaming the sketch for pipe flow velocity profiles

8. Create a new sketch by clicking on **Front Plane** in the **FeatureManager design tree.** Draw a 4600 mm long horizontal line in the x-direction starting at the origin of the pipe. Set the **Parameters** and **Additional Parameters** to the values shown in the figure and close the dialog

    . Rename the sketch in the **FeatureManager design tree** and call it x = 0 – 4.6 m (centerline). Repeat this step but draw the line along the wall of the pipe and name the sketch x = 0 – 4.6 m (wall). Save the SolidWorks part with the following name: **Pipe Flow**.

Figure 6.8a) Adding a line in the x-direction along the centerline of the pipe

Figure 6.8b) Adding a line in the x-direction along the wall of the pipe

Setting up the Flow Simulation Project

9. If Flow Simulation is not available in the menu, you have to add it from SolidWorks menu: **Tools>>Add Ins…** and check the corresponding **SolidWorks Flow Simulation** box. Select **Flow Simulation>>Project>>Wizard** to create a new Flow Simulation project. Create a new figuration named "**Pipe Flow Study**". Click on the **Next >** button. Select the default **SI (m-kg-s)** unit system and click on the **Next>** button once again.

Figure 6.9a) Starting a new Flow Simulation project

Figure 6.9b) Creating a name for the project

10. Use the default **Internal Analysis type**. Click on the **Next >** button.

Figure 6.10 Internal analysis

11. Click on the **New...** button in the **Default Fluid** window to open the **Engineering Database**. Expand **Materials** in the **Database tree** by clicking on the plus sign next to the materials folder. Expand **Gases** and click on **Pre-Defined**. Select **Air** from the list of **Pre-Defined Items**, right click and select **Copy**. Click on **User Defined Gases** in the **Database tree**, right click in the field under the **Items** tab and paste **Air**. Right click on the pasted **Air** and select **Item Properties**. Change the **Dynamic viscosity** to **0.0012 Pa*s** and change the name to the one shown in figure 6.11e). Select **File>>Save** from the **Engineering Database** menu. Close the **Engineering Database** window and add the new fluid as **Project Fluid**. Select **Laminar Only** from the **Flow Type** drop down menu. Click on the **Next >** button. Use the default **Wall Conditions** and **0.5 m/s** for **Velocity in X direction** as **Initial Condition**. Slide the **Result resolution** to **8**. Click on the **Finish** button.

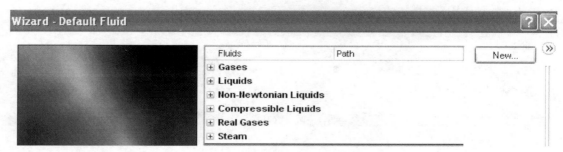

Figure 6.11a) Opening the engineering database

Figure 6.11b) Selecting
pre-defined gases

Figure 6.11c) Copying the pre-defined air

Figure 6.11d) Pasting air to user defined gases

Figure 6.11e) Defining the dynamic viscosity

Creating Lids for the Pipe

12. Select **Flow Simulation>>Tools>>Create Lids…**. Click on **View Orientation** in the graphics window and select **Left** view. Click on the face between the two circles and click on the **D1** button and adjust the thickness of the lid to **1.00 mm**. Close the **Create Lids** dialog ✏️. Answer yes to the question if you want to reset the mesh settings.

Figure 6.12a) Creating a lid for the pipe

Figure 6.12b) Selection of left view for the lid   Figure 6.12c) Adjusting the thickness of the lid

13. Repeat step 12 one more time but select the **Right** view and create a lid with the same thickness for the other end of the pipe. Answer yes to the question if you want to reset the computational domain and also yes to the next question if you want to reset mesh settings.

Figure 6.13 Selection of right view for the second lid

Modifying the Computational Domain and Mesh

14. Select **Flow Simulation>>Computational Domain….** Click on the **Boundary Condition** tab and select **Symmetry** boundary conditions **At Y min:** and **At Z min:** from the drop down menu. Click on the **Size** tab and set both **Y min:** and **Z min:** to **0 m**. Click on the **OK** button to exit the **Computational Domain** window.

Figure 6.14a) Modifying the computational domain

Figure 6.14b) Selecting symmetry boundary conditions

Figure 6.14c) Setting the size of the computational domain

15. Select **Flow Simulation>>Initial Mesh…**. Uncheck the **Automatic setting** box at the bottom of the window. Change the **Number of cells per X:** to **100** and set both **Number of cells per Y:** and **Number of cells per Z:** to **15**. Click on the **OK** button to exit the **Initial Mesh** window.

Figure 6.15a) Modifying the initial mesh

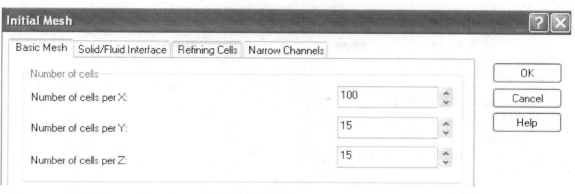

Figure 6.15b) Changing the number of cells

Inserting Boundary Conditions

16. Select the ⬚ **Flow Simulation analysis tree** tab, open the **Input Data** folder by clicking on the plus sign next to it and right click on **Boundary Conditions**. Select **Insert Boundary Condition…**. Select **Front View** from the **View Orientation** drop down menu in the graphics window. Right click in the graphics window and select **Zoom/Pan/Rotate>>Zoom to Area**. Zoom in on the left end of the pipe, right click in the graphics window and select **Zoom/Pan/Rotate>>Rotate View**. Click and drag the mouse so that the inner surface of the inflow boundary is visible. You might have to zoom to area once again to get a close view. Right click one more time with the arrow over the inflow region and click on **Select Other**. Select the surface of the inflow boundary. Select **Inlet Velocity** in the **Type** portion of the **Boundary Condition** window and set the velocity to **0.5 m/s** in the **Flow Parameters** window. Click **OK**
✓ to exit the window. Right click in the graphics window and select 🔍 **Zoom to Area** and select an area around the left boundary.

Figure 6.16a) Inserting boundary condition   Figure 6.16b) Modifying the view

Figure 6.16c) Including a velocity boundary condition on the inflow

Figure 6.16d) Inlet velocity boundary condition indicated by arrows

17. Red arrows pointing in the right direction appears indicating the inlet velocity boundary condition, see figure 6.16d). Right click in the graphics window and select **Zoom to Fit**. Select **Front View** from the **View Orientation** drop down menu in the graphics window. Right click in the graphics window and select **Zoom to Area**. Zoom in on the right end of the pipe.

Right click again in the graphics window and select **Rotate View** once again to rotate the pipe so that the inner right surface is visible in the graphics window. Right click and click on **Select**. Right click on **Boundary Conditions** in the **Flow Simulation analysis tree** and select **Insert Boundary Condition….** Right click one more time over the outflow region and click on **Select Other**. Select the surface of the outflow boundary. Click on the **Pressure Openings** button in the **Type** portion of the **Boundary Condition** window and select **Static Pressure**. Click OK to exit the window.

If you zoom in on the outlet boundary you will see blue arrows indicating the static pressure boundary condition, see figure 6.17b).

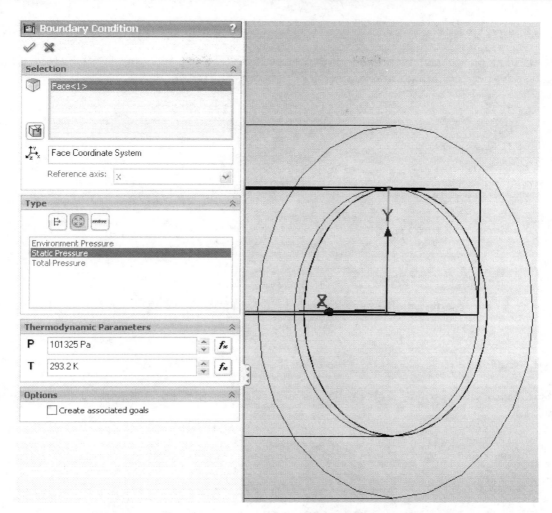

Figure 6.17a) Selection of static pressure as boundary condition at the outlet of the flow region

Figure 6.17b) Outlet static pressure boundary condition

Inserting a Global Goal

18. Right click on **Goals** in the **Flow Simulation analysis tree** and select **Insert Global Goals…**. Select **Max X – Component of Velocity** as a global goal.

Figure 6.18a) Inserting global goals   Figure 6.18b) Selection of X – component of velocity

Running the Calculations for Laminar Pipe Flow

19. Select **Flow Simulation>>Solve>>Run** to start calculations. Click on the **Run** button in the **Run** window.

Figure 6.19a) Starting calculations

Figure 6.19b) Run window

Figure 6.19c) Solver window

Inserting Cut Plots

20. Right click on Cut Plots in the Flow Simulation analysis tree and select Insert....

Select the Front Plane from the FeatureManager design tree. Click on View Settings....

Slide the Number of colors: slide bar to 101. Click on OK. Click OK to exit the Cut Plot window. Rename the cut plot to Pressure. Repeat this step but select X-velocity from the Parameter: drop down menu in the View Settings window. Rename the cut plot to X-velocity. Figure 6.20a) shows the pressure gradient along the length of the pipe. Figure 6.20b) is showing the velocity distribution in the pipe.

Figure 6.20a) Pressure distribution along the straight pipe

Figure 6.20b) Velocity distribution in the inlet section of the straight pipe

Inserting XY Plots for Laminar Pipe Flow using Templates

21. Place the files "**xy-plot figure 6.21c)**", "**xy-plot figure 6.22**" and "**xy-plot figure 6.23**" into the **Local Disk (C:)/Program Files/SolidWorks (2)/SolidWorks Flow Simulation/ /lang/english/template/XY-plots** folder to make it available in the **Template** list.

Click on the FeatureManager design tree. Click on the sketch **x = 0, D, 2D, 3D, 4D, 23D**.

Click on the Flow Simulation analysis tree tab. Right click **XY Plot** and select **Insert….** Check the **X-velocity** box. Open the **Resolution** portion of the **XY Plot** window and slide the **Geometry Resolution** as far as it goes to the right. Click on the **Evenly Distribute Output Points** button and increase the number of points to **500**. Open the **Options** portion of the **XY Plot** window and select the file **xy-plot figure 6.21c).xlt** from the **Template** drop down menu. Click OK to exit the **XY Plot** window. An Excel file will open with a graph of the velocity in the pipe at different streamwise positions, see figure 6.21c).

Figure 6.21a) Selecting the sketch   Figure 6.21b) Different settings for the XY Plot

Figure 6.21c) Straight pipe velocity profiles at different streamwise positions, full line represents theoretical parabolic velocity profile and the Reynolds number is $Re = 100$

In figure 6.21c) the different velocity profiles are compared with the theoretical Hagen-Poiseuille velocity profile for laminar flow in a straight pipe:

$$u_{laminar} = U_{max}(1 - (\tfrac{2y}{D})^2) \qquad\qquad (1)$$

where y (m) is the radial coordinate, u (m/s) is the velocity in the X-direction, and D (m) is the inner diameter of the pipe. We see in figure 6.21c) that the profiles at different streamwise positions further away from the inlet get closer to the fully developed theoretical profile. The theoretical ratio between maximum velocity U_{max} (m/s) and mean velocity U_m (m/s) for fully developed laminar pipe flow is

$$(\tfrac{U_{max}}{U_m})_{laminar} = 2 \qquad\qquad (2)$$

22. Repeat step 21 but this time choose the sketch **x = 0 – 4.6 m (centerline)** and use the template **"xy-plot figure 6.22.xlt"**. This results in figure 6.22 that shows the streamwise development of the centerline velocity. It takes approximately 10 pipe diameters for the flow to become fully developed.

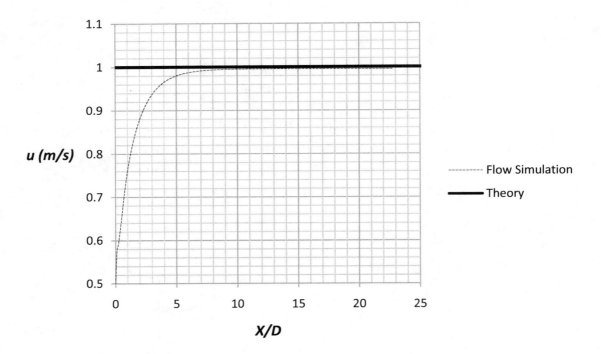

Figure 6.22 X-velocity along the centerline of the pipe at $Re = 100$, full line is showing theoretical value for fully developed flow

Theory for Laminar Pipe Flow

The Reynolds number for the flow in a straight pipe is defined as

$$Re = \frac{U_m D}{\nu} \qquad (3)$$

where ν is the kinematic viscosity of the fluid. The hydrodynamic entry length L_h (m) is the distance between the pipe entrance and the location where the flow is fully developed. The entry length is approximately given by the following expression for laminar flow in a pipe:

$$\frac{L_{h,laminar}}{D} = 0.05 Re \qquad (4)$$

In our case, $D = 0.2$ m and $Re = 100$ gives an entry length of 1 m. If we define the entry length as the distance from the entrance to where the streamwise velocity maximum is within 2% of the fully developed value, Flow Simulation results in figure 6.22 gives a value of 1.013 m, only a 1.3 % difference from theoretical results.

We now want to study pressure loss and how the friction factor varies along the pipe. The pressure loss is defined by

$$\Delta P = f \frac{L}{D} \frac{\rho U_m^2}{2}$$

where L (m) is the length of the pipe and ρ (kg/m³) is the density of the fluid. The Darcy-Weisbach friction factor f is defined as:

$$f = \frac{8\tau_w}{\rho U_m^2} \qquad (5)$$

where τ_w (Pa) is the wall shear stress. The Fanning friction factor is defined as:

$$C_f = \frac{\tau_w}{\frac{1}{2}\rho U_m^2} = \frac{f}{4} \qquad (6)$$

For laminar flow in a circular pipe it can be shown that

$$C_{f,laminar} = \frac{16}{Re} \qquad (7)$$

23. Repeat step 21 but this time choose the sketch **x = 0 – 4.6 m (wall)** and check the box for **Shear Stress**. Use template "**xy-plot figure 6.23.xlt**". An Excel file will open with a graph of the Fanning friction factor versus the X/D –coordinate in comparison with theoretical values for laminar pipe flow, see figure 6.23.

Figure 6.23 Fanning friction factor as a function of the streamwise coordinate at $Re = 100$, full line is showing theoretical value for fully developed flow

Running Calculations for Turbulent Pipe Flow

24. In the next step, we will study turbulent pipe flow. Open the file **Turbulent Pipe Flow**.

Select **Flow Simulation>>Solve>>Run** to start calculations. Check the **Mesh** box and select **New Calculation**. Click on the **Run** button in the **Run** window.

Figure 6.24a) Creation of mesh and starting a new calculation for turbulent pipe flow

Figure 6.24b) Solver window for turbulent pipe flow calculations

Theory for Turbulent Pipe Flow

25. An approximate relation for the Darcy-Weisbach friction factor as a function of Reynolds number for turbulent pipe flow is given by Blasius:

$$f_{turbulent} = \frac{0.316}{Re^{1/4}} \qquad 4000 < Re < 10^5 \qquad (8)$$

and the Fanning friction factor

$$C_{f,turbulent} = \frac{0.079}{Re^{1/4}} \qquad 4000 < Re < 10^5 \qquad (9)$$

The pressure drop is given by

$$\Delta P_{turbulent} = 0.158 L \rho^{3/4} \mu^{1/4} U_m^{7/4} / D^{5/4} \qquad (10)$$

where μ is the dynamic viscosity of the fluid. A formula can also be obtained relating max velocity to mean velocity for fully developed turbulent pipe flow:

$$\left(\frac{U_{max}}{U_m}\right)_{turbulent} = 1 + 2.66\sqrt{C_{f,turbulent}} \qquad (11)$$

Inserting XY Plots for Turbulent Pipe Flow using Templates

Place the files "**xy-plot figure 6.25a)**", "**xy-plot figure 6.25b)**", "**xy-plot figure 6.25c)**" and "**xy-plot figure 6.25d)**" into the **Local Disk (C:)/Program Files/SolidWorks (2)/SolidWorks Flow Simulation/ /lang/english/template/XY-plots** folder to make it available in the **Template** list.

Click on the ⬡ **FeatureManager design tree**. Click on the sketch **x = 0 – 10 m (centerline)**.

Click on the ◉ **Flow Simulation analysis tree** tab. Right click **XY Plot** and select **Insert….** Check the **X-velocity** box. Open the **Resolution** portion of the **XY Plot** window and slide the **Geometry Resolution** as far as it goes to the right. Select the template "**xy-plot figure 6.25a)**" from the drop down menu. Click OK ✔ to exit the **XY Plot** window. An Excel file will open with a graph of the velocity along the centerline of the pipe, see figure 6.25a).

Figure 6.25a) is showing the X-velocity along the centerline including a comparison between turbulent pipe flow and the empirical value for fully developed flow. The centerline velocity from Flow Simulation has an overshoot before attaining a level lower than the value given from empirical data. It is clearly seen that Flow Simulation is under predicting the fully developed maximum velocity.

The Fanning friction factor is shown in figure 6.25b). Repeat the steps above to get this graph. Select the sketch **x = 0 – 10 m (wall)** and check the **Shear Stress** box. Select the template "**xy-plot figure 6.25b)**". An Excel file will open with a graph of the friction coefficient along the wall of the pipe, see figure 6.25b). The Fanning factor from Flow Simulation is slightly lower that the empirical value in the region 6 < X/D < 26 and slightly higher further downstream.

Repeat the steps above once again. Select the sketch **x = 45D**. Check the **X-velocity** box. Click on the ✎ **Evenly Distribute Output Points** button and increase the number of points to **500**. Select the template "**xy-plot figure 6.25c)**". In figure 6.25c) is the fully developed velocity profile from Flow Simulation compared with the power-law profile for *n* = 8.

$$u_{turbulent} = U_{max}(1 - \frac{y}{0.1})^{1/n} \qquad (12)$$

Figure 6.25a) X-velocity along the centerline of the pipe at $Re = 100000$, full line is showing empirical value for fully developed turbulent pipe flow

Figure 6.25b) Fanning friction factor as a function of the streamwise coordinate at $Re = 100000$, full line is showing empirical value for fully developed turbulent pipe flow

Figure 6.25c) Fully developed straight pipe turbulent velocity profile (dashed line) at $X/D = 45$, $Re = 100000$, compared with power-law velocity profile for $n = 8$

There are four different layers of the turbulent velocity profile: viscous sublayer, buffer layer, overlap layer and turbulent layer. If we start with the viscous sublayer located closest to the wall, the velocity profile in this region is described by the law of the wall:

$$u^+ = \frac{u}{u_*} = \frac{(\frac{D}{2}-y)u_*}{v} = y^+ \tag{13}$$

where the friction velocity $u_* = \sqrt{\tau_w/\rho}$. The thickness of the viscous sublayer is

$$\delta = \frac{5v}{u_*} \tag{14}$$

The velocity profile in the overlap layer is known as the logarithmic law

$$u^+ = 2.5 ln y^+ + 5.0 \tag{15}$$

and the profile in the outer turbulent layer is called the velocity defect law.

$$\frac{u_{max}-u}{u_*} = 2.5 ln \frac{D}{D-2y} \tag{16}$$

Click on the 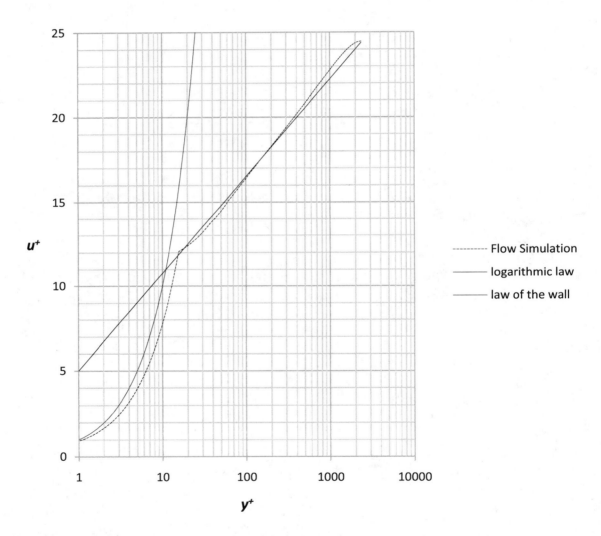 FeatureManager design tree. Click on the sketch **x = 45D**. Click on the
Flow Simulation analysis tree tab. Right click **XY Plot** and select **Insert…**. Check the **X-velocity** box. Open the **Resolution** portion of the **XY Plot** window and slide the **Geometry Resolution** as far as it goes to the right. Click on the **Evenly Distribute Output Points** button and increase the number of points to **10000**. Select the template **"xy-plot figure 6.25d)"** from the drop down menu. Click OK to exit the **XY Plot** window.

In figure 6.25d) it is seen that result from Flow Simulation is under predicting the velocity in the viscous sublayer close to the wall but over predicting the velocity further away from the wall in the overlap and turbulent layers.

Figure 6.25d) Comparison of Flow Simulation, law of the wall and logarithmic law for fully developed turbulent flow in a pipe at $X/D = 45$ and $Re = 100000$

References

[1] SolidWorks Flow Simulation 2009 Technical Reference

[2] White, F. M., Fluid Mechanics, 4th Edition, McGraw-Hill, 1999.

Exercises

1. Run the laminar flow case for $Re = 300$, 500 and compare X-velocity and friction factor with $Re = 100$ as shown in figures 6.22 and 6.23, respectively.

2. Run the laminar flow case for $Re = 100$ and change the number of cells in the X, Y, and Z directions to see how it affects the results.

3. Run the turbulent flow case for $Re = 100000$ and change the number of cells in the X, Y, and Z directions to see how it affects the results.

Notes:

Chapter 7   Flow across a Tube Bank

Objectives

- Creating the SolidWorks model of the tube bank
- Setting up Flow Simulation projects for external flow
- Inserting boundary condition
- Running the calculations
- Using cut plots and XY plots to visualize the resulting flow field
- Compare results with theory and empirical data

Problem Description

In this chapter, we will use Flow Simulation to study the two-dimensional flow across a tube bank. We will use a total of twelve 20 mm diameter cylinders in an in-line arrangement. The cylinders will have a temperature of 373.2 K and the free stream velocity of the air will be 4 m/s. The temperature and velocity fields will be shown inside the tube bank and the development of both temperature and velocity profiles after the tube bank. The exit temperature of the fluid from Flow Simulation calculations will be compared with theoretical and empirical results.

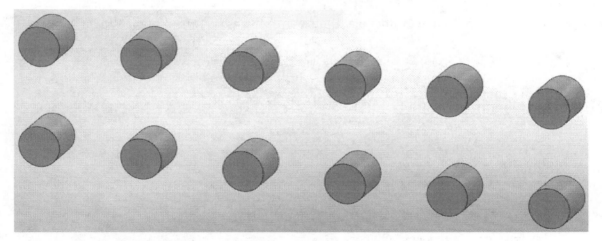

Figure 7.0 SolidWorks model of in-line tube bank

Creating the SolidWorks Part

1. Start by creating a new part in SolidWorks: select **File>>New** and click on the **OK** button in the **New SolidWorks Document** window. Click on **Front Plane** in the **FeatureManager design tree** and select **Front** from the **View Orientation** drop down menu in the graphics window.

Figure 7.1a) Selection of front plane

Figure 7.1b) Selection of right view

2. Click on **Circle** from the **Sketch** tools tab.

Figure 7.2 Selecting a sketch tool

3. Click at the origin in the graphics window and create a circle with a radius of 10 mm. Fill in the **Parameters** for the circle as shown in figure 7.3. Close the **Circle** dialog box by clicking on ✓.

Figure 7.3 A circle with a radius of 10 mm

4. Create five more circles with the same radii and their centers located at (X,Y) = (50,0), (100,0), (150,0), (200,0) and (250,0). Next, create another line of six more similar circles with their centers at (X,Y) = (0,50), (50,50), (100,50), (150,50), (200,50) and (250,50). All dimensions in millimeter.

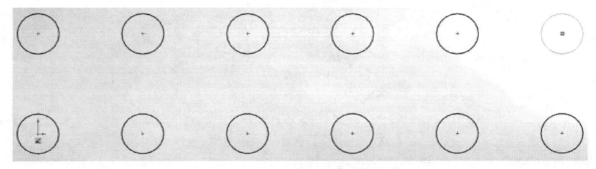

Figure 7.4 Sketch of in-line tube bank with six rows of cylinders

5. Select the **Features** tab and the **Extruded Boss/Base**. Click on **Direction 2** check box and click OK ✓ to exit the **Extrude** dialog box. Select **File>>Save As...** and save the part with the name "**In-Line Tube Bank**".

Figure 7.5a) Selection of extruded boss/base feature

Figure 7.5b) Extruding the sketch

Setting up the Flow Simulation Project

6. If Flow Simulation is not available in the menu, you have to add it from SolidWorks menu: **Tools>>Add Ins...** and check the corresponding **SolidWorks Flow Simulation** box. Select **Flow Simulation>>Project>>Wizard** to create a new Flow Simulation project. Create a new figuration named "**In-Line Tube Bank Study**". Click on the **Next >** button. Select the default **SI (m-kg-s)** unit system and click on the **Next>** button once again.

Figure 7.6a) Starting a new Flow Simulation project

Figure 7.6b) Creating a name for the project

7. Use the **External Analysis type**. Click on the **Next >** button.

Figure 7.7 External analysis type

8. Add **Air** from **Gases** as the **Project Fluid**. Click on the **Next >** button. Use the default **Wall Conditions**. Click on the **Next >** button. Set the **Velocity in X-direction** to **4 m/s**. Click on the **Next >** button. Use the **Result resolution** at level **3**. Click on the **Finish** button.

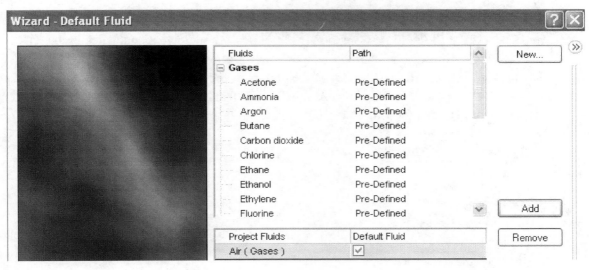

Figure 7.8a) Adding air as the project fluid

Figure 7.8b) Setting the velocity in the X-direction

Figure 7.8c) Setting the result resolution

Modifying the Computational Domain and Mesh

9. Select **Flow Simulation>>Computational Domain…**. Click on the **Boundary Condition** tab and select **XY – Plane Flow** from the **2D plane flow:** drop down menu. Click on the **OK** button to exit the **Computational Domain** window. Select **Flow Simulation>>Initial Mesh…**. Uncheck the **Automatic setting** box at the bottom of the window. Change the **Number of cells per X:** to **198** and set **Number of cells per Y:** to **300** and **Number of cells per Z:** to **1**. Click on the **OK** button to exit the **Initial Mesh** window.

Figure 7.9a) Modifying the computational domain

Figure 7.9b) Selecting 2D plane flow

Figure 7.9c) Modifying initial mesh

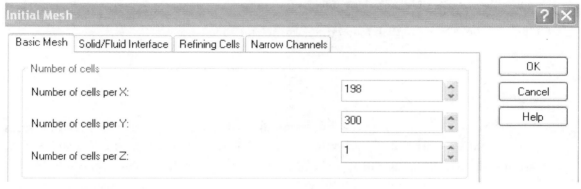

Figure 7.9d) Setting the number of cells

Inserting Boundary Conditions

10. Select **Isometric** view from the **View Orientation** drop down menu in the graphics window. Select **Flow Simulation>>Insert>>Boundary Condition….** Select the twelve cylindrical surfaces. Click on the ⌐⌐ **Wall** button in the **Type** portion of the **Boundary Condition** window and select **Real Wall**. Adjust the **Wall Temperature** to **373.2 K** by clicking on the button and enter the numerical value in the **Wall Parameters** window. Click OK to exit the **Boundary Condition** window.

Figure 7.10a) Selecting an isometric view

Figure 7.10b) Selection of cylindrical surfaces

Figure 7.10c) Selecting wall temperature for in-line tube bank

Inserting Global Goals

11. Right click on **Goals** in the **Flow Simulation analysis tree** and select **Insert Global Goals…**. Select **Max X – Component of Velocity** as a global goal. Also select **Min, Av** and **Max Temperature of Fluid** as global goals. Click OK ✔ to exit the **Global Goals** window.

Figure 7.11 Selection of X – component of velocity and temperature of fluid as global goals

Running the Calculations for Tube Bank Flow

12. Select **Flow Simulation>>Solve>>Run** to start calculations. Click on the **Run** button in the **Run** window.

Figure 7.12a) Starting calculations   Figure 7.12b) Run window

Figure 7.12c) Solver window

Inserting Cut Plots

13. Right click on Cut Plots in the Flow Simulation analysis tree and select **Insert....** Select the **Front Plane** from the FeatureManager design tree. Click on View Settings... . Slide the **Number of colors:** slide bar to **101**. Click on OK . Click OK to exit the **Cut Plot** window. Name the cut plot as **Pressure**. Select **Front** from the **View Orientation** drop down menu in the graphics window. Repeat this step two more times but select **X-velocity** and **Temperature** as **Parameters** in the **View Settings** window. Figure 7.13a) shows the pressure gradient along the tube bank. Figure 7.13b) is showing the velocity distribution in the same cross section and figure 7.13c) is showing the temperature distribution.

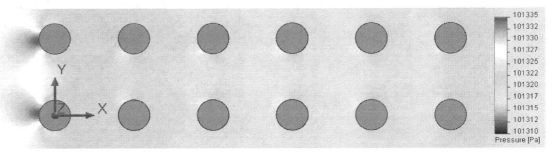

Figure 7.13a) Pressure distribution along the tube bank

Figure 7.13b) Velocity distribution along the tube bank

Figure 7.13c) Temperature distribution along the tube bank

Creating Sketch for XY Plots

14. Click on the 🔖 **FeatureManager design tree** and select the **Front Plane**. Click on the **Sketch** tools tab and select **Line**. Draw a 50 mm long vertical line starting at $(X, Y) = (275 \text{ mm}, 0)$, see figure 7.14a). Exit the **Line Properties** window and draw two more vertical lines with the same length starting at $(X, Y) = (300 \text{ mm}, 0)$ and $(X, Y) = (325 \text{ mm}, 0)$. Close the **Insert Line** window

and select 🔘 **Rebuild** from the SolidWorks Menu. Rename the new sketch to the name **x = 275, 300, 325 mm** as shown in figure 7.14d).

Place the files "**xy-plot figure 7.14f)**" and "**xy-plot figure 7.14g)**" into the **Local Disk (C:)/Program Files/SolidWorks (2)/SolidWorks Flow Simulation /lang/english/template/XY-Plots** folder to make it available in the **Template** list.

Click on the [icon] **Flow Simulation analysis tree** tab. Right click **XY Plot** and select **Insert…**. Check the **Temperature** box. Open the **Resolution** portion of the **XY Plot** window and slide the **Geometry Resolution** as far as it goes to the right. Open the **Options** portion of the **XY Plot** window and select the template **xy-plot figure 7.14f)** from the template drop down menu. Click on the [icon] **FeatureManager design tree** and select the sketch **x = 275, 300, 325 mm**. Click OK [icon] to exit the **XY Plot** window. An Excel file will open with a graph of the temperature across the exit of the tube bank, see figure 7.14f). Repeat this step once again but choose to check the **X-velocity** box and select the **xy-plot figure 7.14g)** template.

Figure 7.14a) Drawing a vertical line for the XY-plot   Figure 7.14b) Rebuilding the new sketch

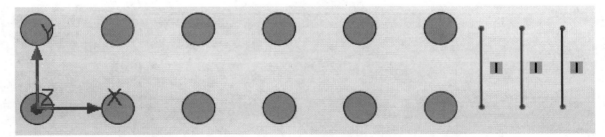

Figure 7.14c) Sketch with three lines for temperature profiles

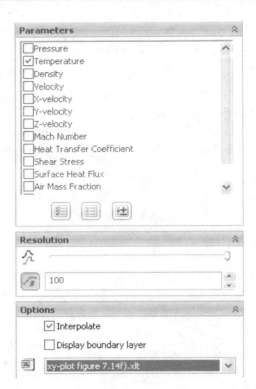

Figure 7.14d) Rename the new sketch   Figure 7.14e) Different settings for XY Plot

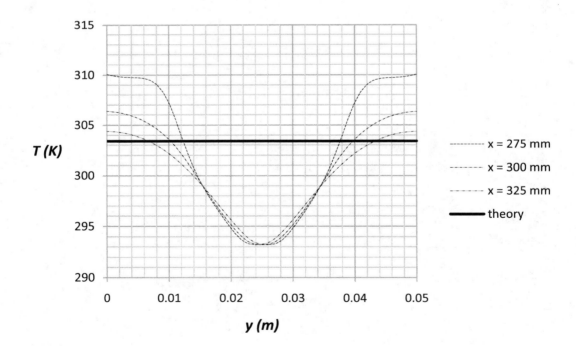

Figure 7.14f) Exit temperatures for the tube bank from Flow Simulation compared with calculations (full line)

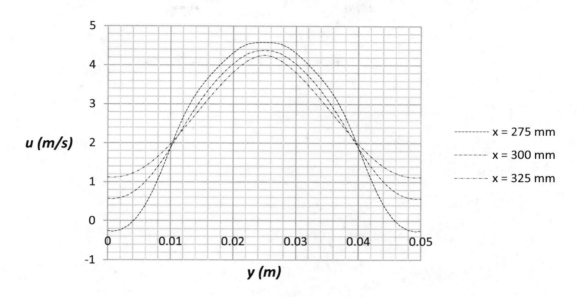

7.14g) Exit velocities for the tube bank from Flow Simulation

Theory and Empirical Data

15. The Reynolds number for a tube bank is defined based on the maximum velocity U_{max} (m/s) in the bank:

$$Re_{D,max} = \frac{U_{max}D}{\nu}$$ (1)

where D (m) is the diameter of the tubes and ν (m/s) is the kinematic viscosity of the fluid.

Figure 7.15a) Geometry of in-line tube bank

For the in-line tube arrangement, see figure 7.15a), the maximum velocity is related to the approach velocity U:

$$U_{max} = \frac{S_T U}{S_T - D}$$ (2)

For the staggered tube arrangement, see figure 7.15b), the maximum velocity is determined by equation (2) if $2A_D > A_T$. If $2A_D < A_T$, the maximum velocity is determined by

$$U_{max} = \frac{S_T U}{2(S_D - D)} \qquad (3)$$

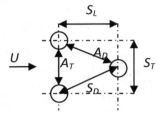

Figure 7.15b) Geometry of staggered tube bank

The pressure drop across the tube bank is given by the following equation:

$$\Delta P = \frac{N_L f \chi \rho U_{max}^2}{2} \qquad (4)$$

where N_L is the number of rows of tubes in the flow direction, f is the friction factor, χ is a correction factor and ρ (kg/m^3) is the density of the fluid.

The friction factor for in-line and staggered tube banks can be determined from figures 7.15c) and 7.15d), respectively.

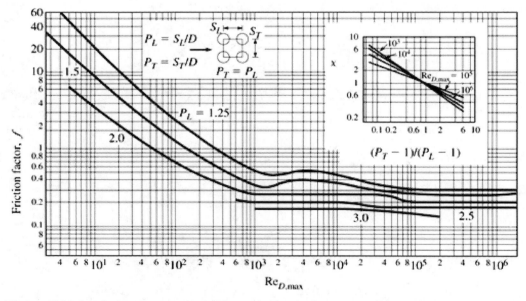

Figure 7.15c) Friction factors for in-line tube bank, from Cengel (2003)

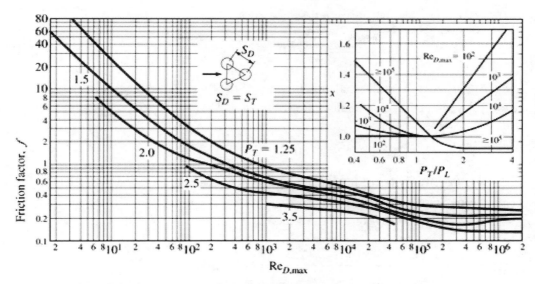

Figure 7.15d) Friction factors for staggered tube bank, from Cengel (2003)

In this case we are using a square in-line tube bank so the correction factor $\chi = 1$. The maximum velocity is

$$U_{max} = \frac{S_T U}{S_T - D} = \frac{0.050m \cdot 4m/s}{0.050m - 0.020m} = 6.67 \ m/s \tag{5}$$

The Reynolds number can be determined based on an assumed mean temperature of 25°C based on the average of the inlet and outlet temperatures:

$$Re_{D,max} = \frac{U_{max} D}{\nu} = \frac{6.67m/s \cdot 0.020m}{1.562 \cdot 10^{-5} m^2/s} = 8536 \tag{6}$$

The average Nusselt number Nu for six rows of in-line tubes in the flow direction

$$Nu = 0.27 F Re_{D,max}^{0.63} Pr^{0.36} \left(\frac{Pr}{Pr_s}\right)^{0.25} = 0.27 \cdot 0.945 \cdot 8536^{0.63} \cdot 0.7296^{0.36} \left(\frac{0.7296}{0.7073}\right)^{0.25} = 68.8$$

where Pr and Pr_s are the Prandtl numbers at the mean and surface temperature, respectively and F is a correction factor used for $N_L < 16$ and $Re_{D,max} > 1000$.

Figure 7.15e) Correction factors F for in-line (full line) and staggered (dashed line) tube banks

The average heat transfer coefficient h then becomes

$$h = \frac{kNu}{D} = \frac{0.02551 W/(m \cdot °C) \cdot 68.8}{0.02\ m} = 87.75\ W/(m^2 \cdot °C) \tag{7}$$

where $k\ (W/(m^2 \cdot °C))$ is the thermal conductivity of the fluid. The exit temperature T_e (°C) of the fluid can be determined from the inlet temperature T_i (°C) and the surface temperature T_s (°C)

$$T_e = T_s - (T_s - T_i)e^{\frac{-hN_L \pi D}{\rho U S_T C_P}} = 100°C - (100°C - 20°C)e^{\frac{-87.75 \cdot 6\pi \cdot 0.02}{1.204 \cdot 4 \cdot 0.05 \cdot 1007}} = 30.2\ °C$$

where $C_P\ (J/(kg \cdot °C))$ is the specific heat of the air. The average temperature as determined from Flow Simulation results, see figure 7.14f) at x = 300 mm is 30.23 °C, almost identical to the result above. Finally, the pressure drop is determined to be

$$\Delta P = \frac{N_L f \chi \rho U_{max}^2}{2} = \frac{6 \cdot 0.2 \cdot 1 \cdot 1.184\left(\frac{kg}{m^3}\right) \cdot 6.67^2 \frac{m^2}{s}}{2} = 31.6\ Pa \tag{8}$$

Reference

[1] Çengel, Y. A., Heat Transfer: A Practical Approach, 2nd Edition, McGraw-Hill, 2003.

Exercises

1. Change the mesh resolution in the flow simulations and see how the mesh size affects the maximum velocity and temperature profiles as shown in figures 7.14f) and 7.14g).

2. Use an in-line five rows, $N_L = 5$, tube grid for flow simulations with a rectangular arrangement $S_L = 2S_T$, see figure 7.15a) and compare exit temperatures with corresponding calculations.

3. Use a staggered grid for flow simulations with $S_L = S_T$, see figure 7.15b) and compare exit temperature profiles with corresponding calculations as shown in this chapter for in-line arrangement. For a staggered arrangement the Nusselt number in the range of Reynolds numbers $Re = 1,000 - 200,000$ is given by

$$Nu = 0.35F(S_T/S_L)^{0.2}Re_{D,max}^{0.6}Pr^{0.36}\left(\frac{Pr}{Pr_s}\right)^{0.25} \tag{9}$$

4. Use a staggered grid for flow simulations with $S_L = 2S_T$, see figure 7.15b) and compare exit temperature profiles with corresponding calculations.

Chapter 8   Heat Exchanger

Objectives

- Creating the SolidWorks model of the heat exchanger
- Setting up Flow Simulation projects for internal flow
- Creating lids for the model
- Inserting boundary conditions
- Running the calculations
- Inserting surface parameters
- Using cut plots to visualize the resulting flow field
- Compare Flow Simulation results with effectiveness – NTU method

Problem Description

In this chapter, we will use SolidWorks Flow Simulation to study the flow in a stainless steel parallel flow shell and tube heat exchanger. Heat transfer will occur between the hot inner tube flow and the colder outer flow in the shell. The shell has a wall thickness of 10 mm and an inner diameter of 32 mm whereas the tube is 2 mm thick and has an outer diameter of 19 mm. The mass flow rate of water in the shell is 0.8 kg/s with an inlet temperature of 283.2 K and the mass flow rate of water in the tube is 0.2 kg/s at an inlet temperature of 343.2 K. The temperature distributions along the shell and tube will be shown from Flow Simulation results and the temperature of the hot water at the tube outlet will be used in comparison with the effectiveness – NTU method for calculation of the effectiveness of the parallel flow shell and tube heat exchanger.

Figure 8.0 SolidWorks model of shell and tube heat exchanger

Creating the SolidWorks Part

1. Start by creating a new part in SolidWorks: select **File>>New** and click on the **OK** button in the **New SolidWorks Document** window. Click on **Front Plane** in the **FeatureManager design tree** and select **Front** from the **View Orientation** drop down menu in the graphics window.

Figure 8.1a) Selection of front plane

Figure 8.1b) Selection of right view

2. Click on **Circle** from the **Sketch** tools tab.

Figure 8.2 Selecting a sketch tool

3. Click at the origin in the graphics window and create a circle with a radius of 16 mm. Fill in the **Parameters** for the circle as shown in figure 8.3. Close the **Circle** dialog box by clicking on **Close Dialog** .

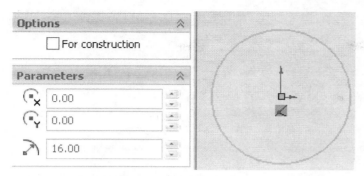

Figure 8.3 A circle with a radius of 16 mm

4. Select the **Features** tab and the **Extruded Boss/Base**. Enter **1000.00mm** for the **Depth D1** of the extrusion in **Direction 1**. Check the **Thin Feature** box and also check the **Cap ends** box. Close the **Extrude** dialog box by clicking on **OK** ✓ . Right click in the graphics window and select **Zoom/Pan/Rotate>>Zoom to Fit**. Select **Left** view from **View Orientation** in the graphics window, see figure 8.4c). Select **Top Plane** from **Featuremanager design tree**. Insert a new plane from the SolidWorks menu by selecting **Insert>>Reference Geometry>>Plane**. Set the **Offset Distance** to **26.00mm** and exit the **Plane** dialog box. Select **Top** view from **View Orientation** in the graphics window, see figure 8.4g).

Figure 8.4a) Selection of extruded boss/base feature   Figure 8.4b) Extruding the sketch

Figure 8.4c) Selecting a left view

Figure 8.4d) Selecting top plane

Figure 8.4e) Inserting a plane

Figure 8.4f) Setting the location of the plane

Figure 8.4g) Selecting top view

5. Right click in the graphics window and select **Zoom/Pan/Rotate>>Zoom to Area**. Select a region in the graphics window around the lower end of the tube. Click on **Plane 1** in the **Featuremanager design tree** and select **Circle** from the **Sketch** tools. Draw a circle with the parameters as given in figure 8.5b). Close the **Circle** dialog box by clicking on **OK** ✓. Select the **Features** tab and **Extruded Cut**. Set the **Depth** of the cut to **26.00mm**. Close the **Extrude** dialog box by clicking on **OK** ✓.

Figure 8.5a) Selecting zoom to area

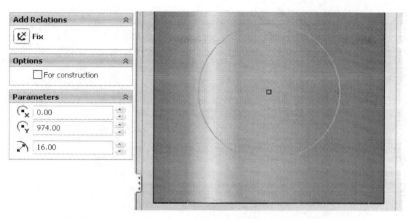

Figure 8.5b) Drawing of a circle for the extrusion.

Figure 8.5c) Selecting the extruded cut tool

Figure 8.5d) Settings for extruded cut

6. Click on the plus sign next to **Extrude 1**, select **Sketch 2** in the **Featuremanager design tree** and click on **Extruded Boss/Base** from **Features**. Set the **Depth D1** of the extrusion in **Direction 1** to **75.00mm**. Check the **Direction 2** box and enter **10.00mm** for the **Depth**. Check the **Thin Feature** box and enter **4.00mm** for the **Thickness**. Close the **Extrude** dialog box.

Figure 8.6a) Selecting sketch 2 and the extruded boss/base feature

Figure 8.6b) Settings for dimensions of the extrusion from plane 1

7. Select **Left** view from **View Orientation** in the graphics window, see figure 8.4c). Select **Top Plane** from **Featuremanager design tree**. Insert a new plane from the SolidWorks menu by selecting **Insert>>Reference Geometry>>Plane**. Set the **Offset Distance** to **26.00mm**, check the **Reverse direction** box and exit the **Plane** dialog box. Select **Bottom** view from **View Orientation** in the graphics window, see figure 8.7a). Right click in the graphics window and select **Zoom/Pan/Rotate>>Zoom to Area**. Select a region in the graphics window around the lower end of the tube. Click on **Plane 2** in the **Featuremanager design tree** and select **Circle** from the **Sketch** tools. Draw a circle with the parameters as given in figure 8.7b). Close the **Circle** dialog box by clicking on **OK** ✓. Select the **Features** tab and **Extruded Cut**. Set the **Depth** of the cut to **26.00mm** and click on the **Reverse Direction** ⬀ button. Close the **Extrude** dialog box by clicking on **OK** ✓.

Figure 8.7a) Bottom view from view orientation

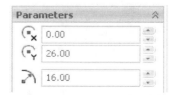

Figure 8.7b) Parameters for circle

8. Click on the plus sign next to **Extrude 2**, select **Sketch 3** in the **Featuremanager design tree** and click on **Extruded Boss/Base** from **Features**. Enter **10.00mm** as the **Depth** for **Direction 1**. Check the **Direction 2** box and enter **75.00mm** for the **Depth**. Check the **Thin Feature** box and enter **4.00mm** for the **Thickness**. Close the **Extrude** dialog box by clicking on **OK** ✓.

Figure 8.8 Extrusion from plane 2

9. Select **Back** view from **View Orientation** in the graphics window, see figure 8.9a). Select **Front Plane** from **Featuremanager design tree**. Select **Circle** from the **Sketch** tools. Draw a circle with the parameters as given in figure 8.9b). Close the **Circle** dialog box by clicking on **OK** ✓. Select the **Features** tab and **Extruded Cut**. Set the **Depth** of the cut to **1000.00mm** and click on the **Reverse Direction** ⟲ button. Close the **Extrude** dialog box by clicking on **OK** ✓.

Figure 8.9a) Selection of back view

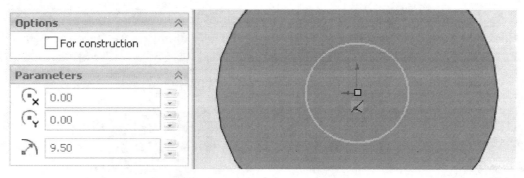

Figure 8.9b) Parameters for circle

Figure 8.9c) Settings for extrusion

10. Click on the plus sign next to **Extrude 3**, select **Sketch 4** in the **Featuremanager design tree** and click on **Extruded Boss/Base** from **Features**. Enter **1026.00mm** as the **Depth** for **Direction 1**. Check the **Direction 2** box and enter **26.00mm** for the **Depth**. Check the **Thin Feature** box, click on the **Reverse Direction** button and enter **2.00mm** for **Thickness**. Close the **Extrude** dialog box by clicking on **OK** . Right click on **Plane 1** in the **Featuremanager design tree** and select **Hide** . Repeat this step for **Plane 2**. Select **Left** view from **View Orientation** in the graphics window, see figure 8.4c). Save the part with the name "**Heat Exchanger Shell and Tube**".

Figure 8.10a) Settings for extrusion from front plane

Figure 8.10b) Hiding planes 1 and 2

Figure 8.10c) Finished shell and tube heat exchanger

Setting up the Flow Simulation Project

11. If Flow Simulation is not available in the menu, you have to add it from SolidWorks menu: Select **Tools>>Add Ins...** and check the corresponding **SolidWorks Flow Simulation** box. Select **Flow Simulation>>Project>>Wizard** to create a new Flow Simulation project. Create a new figuration named "**Shell and Tube Heat Exchanger Study**". Click on the **Next >** button. Select the default **SI (m-kg-s)** unit system and click on the **Next>** button once again.

Figure 11a) Starting a new Flow Simulation project

Figure 8.11b) Creating a name for the project

12. Use the default **Internal Analysis type** and check the **Heat conduction in solids** box. Click on the **Next >** button.

Figure 8.12 Internal analysis type with heat conduction in solids

13. Add **Water** from **Liquids** as the **Project Fluid**. Click on the **Next >** button. Select **Alloys>> Stainless Steel** as the default solid. Click on the **Next >** button. Use the default **Wall Conditions** and the default **Initial Conditions**. Click on the **Next >** button. Use the **Result resolution** of level **3**. Click on the **Finish** button.

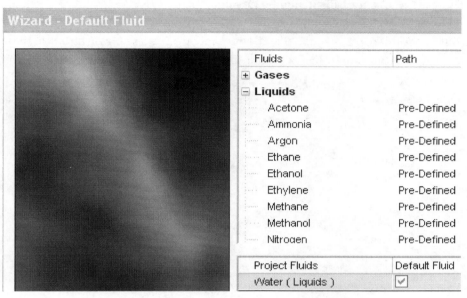

Figure 8.13a) Adding water as the project fluid

Figure 8.13b) Selecting stainless steel as the default solid

Figure 8.13c) Setting the result resolution

Creating Lids

14. Select **Flow Simulation>>Tools>>Create Lids...** from the SolidWorks menu. Select **Back** view from **View Orientation** in the graphics window, see figure 8.9a). Select the face as shown in figure 8.14b). Close the **Create Lids** dialog box by clicking on **OK** ✓ . Answer yes to the question if you want to reset mesh setting. Select **Flow Simulation>>Tools>>Create Lids...** once again from the SolidWorks menu. Select **Front** view from **View Orientation** in the graphics window. Select the similar face as above and close the **Create Lids** dialog box by clicking on **OK** ✓ . Answer yes to the question if you want to reset mesh setting.

Figure 8.14a) Creating a lid

Figure 8.14b) Selecting the face for the lid

15. Select **Flow Simulation>>Tools>>Create Lids...** from the SolidWorks menu. Select **Bottom** view from **View Orientation** in the graphics window. Zoom in on the bottom part of the heat exchanger and select the face as shown in figure 8.15. Close the **Create Lids** dialog box by clicking on **OK** ✎ . Answer yes to the question if you want to reset mesh setting. Select **Flow Simulation>>Tools>>Create Lids...** from the SolidWorks menu. Select **Top** view from **View Orientation** in the graphics window. Zoom in and select the similar face as shown in figure 8.15. Close the **Create Lids** dialog box by clicking on **OK** ✎ . Answer yes to the question if you want to reset mesh setting.

Figure 8.15 Selection of face for third lid

Inserting Boundary Conditions

16. Select **Left** view from **View Orientation** in the graphics window. Right click in the graphics window and select **Zoom/Pan/Rotate>>Rotate View**. Rotate the view and select **Zoom to Area**. Zoom in at the left end of the heat exchanger, see figure 8.16b). Click on the plus sign next to the **Input Data** folder in the **Flow Simulation analysis tree**. Right click on **Boundary Conditions** and select **Insert Boundary Condition…**. Right click on the tube and select **Select Other**. Select the inner surface of the lid, see figure 8.16b). Set the inlet mass flow to **0.2 kg/s** and the **Temperature** to **343.2 K**. Click OK ✓ to exit the **Boundary Condition** window. Rename the created boundary condition in the **Flow Simulation analysis tree** to **Inlet Mass Flow for Tube**.

Figure 8.16a) Selection of rotate view

Figure 8.16b) Selecting face for tube inflow region

Figure 8.16c) Tube inflow parameters

17. Zoom out a little bit and rotate the view a little bit, see figure 8.17a). Right click on **Boundary Conditions** and select **Insert Boundary Condition…**. Right click on the shell and select the inner surface of the shell inflow lid, see figure 8.17a). Set the inlet mass flow to **0.8 kg/s** and the **Temperature** to **283.2 K**. Click OK ✓ to exit the **Boundary Condition** window. Rename the boundary condition to **Inlet Mass Flow for Shell**.

Figure 8.17a) Selecting face for shell inflow region   Figure 8.17b) Shell inflow parameters

18. Select **Left** view from **View Orientation** in the graphics window. Right click in the graphics window and select **Zoom/Pan/Rotate>>Rotate View**. Rotate the view and select **Zoom to Area**. Zoom in at the right end of the heat exchanger, see figure 8.18a). Right click on **Boundary Conditions** and select **Insert Boundary Condition....** Right click on the tube outflow region and click on **Select Other**. Select the inner surface of the lid, see figure 8.18a). Click on the **Pressure Openings** button and select **Environment Pressure**. Click OK to exit the **Boundary Condition** window. Rename the boundary condition to **Environment Pressure for Tube**.

Figure 8.18a) Selecting face for tube outflow region   Figure 8.18b) Tube outflow parameters

19. Right click in the graphics window and select **Zoom/Pan/Rotate>>Rotate View**. Rotate the view a little bit, see figure 8.19a). Right click on **Boundary Conditions** and select **Insert Boundary Condition…**. Right click on the shell outflow region and click on **Select Other**. Select the inner surface of the lid, see figure 8.19b). Click on the **Pressure Openings** button. Click OK ✅ to exit the **Boundary Condition** window. Rename the boundary condition to **Environment Pressure for Shell**.

Figure 8.19a) Rotating the view   Figure 8.19b) Selecting face for shell outflow region

Inserting Goals

20. Right click on **Goals** in the **Flow Simulation analysis tree** and select **Insert Global Goals…**. Select **Min**, **Av** and **Max Temperature of Fluid and Solid** as global goals. Click OK ✅ to exit the **Global Goals** window.

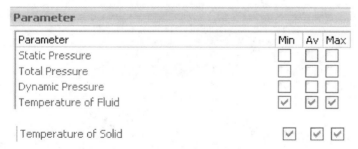

Parameter	Min	Av	Max
Static Pressure	☐	☐	☐
Total Pressure	☐	☐	☐
Dynamic Pressure	☐	☐	☐
Temperature of Fluid	☑	☑	☑
Temperature of Solid	☑	☑	☑

Figure 8.20 Selection of global goals

Running the Calculations for Heat Exchanger

21. Select **Flow Simulation>>Solve>>Run** to start calculations. Click on the **Run** button in the **Run** window.

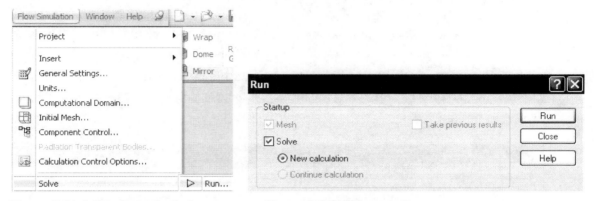

Figure 8.21a) Starting calculations   Figure 8.21b) Run window

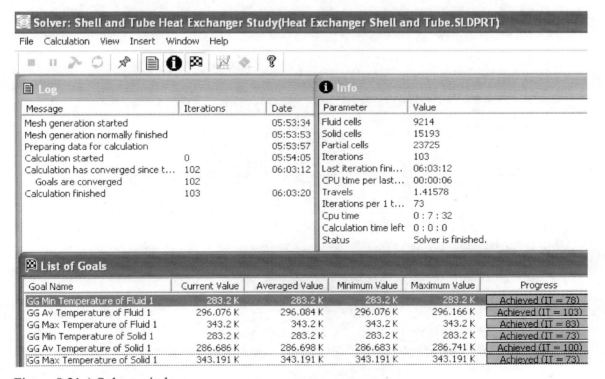

Figure 8.21c) Solver window

Inserting Surface Parameters

22. Right click on **Surface Parameters** in the **Flow Simulation analysis tree** and select **Insert….** Select the **Environment Pressure for Tube Boundary Condition** in the **Flow Simulation analysis tree**. Click on the **Evaluate** button in the **Surface Parameters** window. Select the **Local** tab. The minimum temperature at the tube outflow region is **334.839 K** and the average value is **336.242 K**. Select the **Definition** tab. Select the **Environment Pressure for Shell Boundary Condition** in the **Flow Simulation analysis tree**. Click on the **Evaluate** button in the **Surface Parameters** window. Select the **Local** tab. The average temperature at the shell outflow region is **285 K**.

Figure 8.22 Values of different parameters at the tube outflow region

Inserting Cut Plots

23. Right click on **Cut Plots** in the **Flow Simulation analysis tree** and select **Insert….** Select the **Right Plane** from the **FeatureManager design tree**. Click on **View Settings…**. Slide the **Number of colors:** slide bar to **101**. Select **Temperature** from the **Parameter:** dropdown menu. Set the **Min:** temperature to **334.839 K**. Click on **OK**. Click OK to exit the **Cut Plot** window. Rename the cut plot to **Tube Temperature**.

Click on the **Flow Simulation** tab and the **Geometry** button to display the cut plot. Also, click on the **Lightning** button located above the geometry button. Select **Left** view from **View Orientation** in the graphics window. Repeat this step and insert another cut plot but set the minimum temperature to **283.2 K** and the maximum temperature to **285 K** in order to see the temperature variation of the shell, see figure 8.23c). Rename the cut plot to **Shell Temperature**.

Figure 8.23a) Geometry button in Flow Simulation

Figure 8.23b) Temperature distribution along the tube

Figure 8.23c) Temperature distribution along the shell

Effectiveness – NTU Method

24. We will now use the effectiveness –NTU method for comparison of outlet temperatures with Flow Simulation results. First, we determine the heat capacity rates of the cold and the hot fluids, respectively. The heat capacity rate of the cold C_c and hot C_h fluids are

$$C_c = \dot{m}_c C_{pc} = \frac{0.8 kg}{s} \cdot \frac{4194 J}{kg \cdot K} = 3355.2 \; W/K \tag{1}$$

$$C_h = \dot{m}_h C_{ph} = \frac{0.2 kg}{s} \cdot \frac{4190 J}{kg \cdot K} = 838 \; W/K \tag{2}$$

where $\dot{m}$ is the mass flow rate and C_p is the specific heat. The maximum heat transfer rate is given by

$$\dot{Q}_{max} = C_{min}\left(T_{h,in} - T_{c,in}\right) = C_h\left(T_{h,in} - T_{c,in}\right) = 838 \frac{W}{K} \cdot (343.2 - 283.2)K = 50.28 \; kW$$

where $T_{h,in}$ and $T_{c,in}$ are the hot and cold inflow temperatures, respectively. The heat transfer surface area is

$$A_s = \pi DL = \pi \cdot 0.015m \cdot 0.98m = 0.046 m^2 \tag{3}$$

where D is the inner diameter of the tube and L is the length. The number of transfer units NTU is given by

$$NTU = \frac{U A_s}{C_{min}} \tag{4}$$

where U is the overall heat transfer coefficient. The mean velocities U_m in the hot tube is

$$U_m = \frac{4\dot{m}_h}{\pi \rho D^2} = \frac{4 \cdot 0.2 kg/s}{\pi \cdot 977.5 \frac{kg}{m^3} \cdot 0.015^2 m^2} = 1.158 m/s \tag{5}$$

where ρ is the density of the fluid. The Reynolds number Re for the tube is given by

$$Re = \frac{\rho U_m D}{\mu} = \frac{977.5 \frac{kg}{m^3} \cdot 1.158 \frac{m}{s} \cdot 0.015m}{0.404 \cdot 10^{-3} \frac{kg}{m \cdot s}} = 42{,}021 \tag{6}$$

The flow is turbulent and for smooth tubes the friction factor f can be determined from the Petukhov equation

$$f = \frac{1}{(0.79 ln Re - 1.64)^2} = 0.0218 \qquad 10^4 < Re < 10^6 \tag{7}$$

The Nusselt number Nu is a function of the friction factor, Reynolds number and Prandtl number ($Pr = 2.55$) according to the Gnielinski equation

$$Nu = \frac{(\frac{f}{8})(Re-1000)Pr}{1+12.7(\frac{f}{8})^{\frac{1}{2}}(Pr^{\frac{2}{3}}-1)} = 181.16, \quad 3 \cdot 10^3 < Re < 5 \cdot 10^6, 0.5 \le Pr \le 2000 \quad (8)$$

The convection heat transfer coefficient h for the tube can then be determined from

$$h_i = \frac{kNu}{D} = \frac{0.663\frac{W}{m \cdot K} \cdot 181.16}{0.015m} = 8,007.13 \frac{W}{m^2 \cdot K} \quad (9)$$

For the colder shell the mean velocity is

$$U_m = \frac{4\dot{m}_c}{\pi\rho(D_o^2-D_i^2)} = \frac{4 \cdot 0.8kg/s}{\pi \cdot 999.7\frac{kg}{m^3} \cdot (0.032^2 m^2 - 0.019^2 m^2)} = 1.537 m/s \quad (10)$$

where D_o is the inner diameter of the shell and D_i is the outer diameter of the tube. The Reynolds number for the shell is given by

$$Re = \frac{\rho U_m (D_o - D_i)}{\mu} = \frac{999.7\frac{kg}{m^3} \cdot 1.537\frac{m}{s} \cdot 0.013m}{1.307 \cdot 10^{-3}\frac{kg}{m \cdot s}} = 15,281 \quad (11)$$

This flow is also turbulent $Re > 10,000$ and from eq. (7) we get the friction factor $f = 0.0280$. The Nusselt number from eq. (8) using $Pr = 9.45$ is $Nu = 131.09$ and the convection heat transfer coefficient for the shell

$$h_o = \frac{kNu}{D_o - D_i} = \frac{0.58\frac{W}{m \cdot K} \cdot 131.09}{0.013m} = 5,848.74 \frac{W}{m^2 \cdot K} \quad (12)$$

The thermal resistance R for the shell and tube heat exchanger becomes

$$R = \frac{1}{UA_s} = \frac{1}{\pi L}\left(\frac{1}{h_i D} + \frac{\ln(\frac{D_i}{D})}{2k_{ss}} + \frac{1}{h_o D_i}\right) = 0.00817 K/W \quad (13)$$

where $k_{ss} = 15.1 \, W/(m \cdot K)$ is the thermal conductivity of stainless steel. Equation (4) can now be used to determine $NTU = 0.1461$. The capacity ratio c is given by

$$c = \frac{C_{min}}{C_{max}} = \frac{C_h}{C_c} = 0.25 \quad (14)$$

Finally, the effectiveness of a parallel-flow shell and tube heat exchanger can be determined

$$\epsilon = \frac{1 - e^{-NTU(1+c)}}{1+c} = 0.1335 \quad (15)$$

Using results from Flow Simulation, we get the following effectiveness

$$\epsilon = \frac{T_{h,in} - T_{h,out}}{T_{h,in} - T_{c,in}} = \frac{343.2K - 336.254K}{343.2K - 283.2K} = 0.1158 \quad (16)$$

This is a difference of 13.3% as compared with the effectiveness – NTU method.

References

[1] Çengel, Y. A., Heat Transfer: A Practical Approach, 2nd Edition, McGraw-Hill, 2003.

[2] SolidWorks Flow Simulation 2009 Tutorial

Exercises

1. Change the mesh resolution in flow simulations and see how the mesh size affects the effectiveness of the parallel-flow shell and tube heat exchanger.

2. Use counter-flow instead of parallel-flow for flow simulations and compare effectiveness with corresponding calculations as shown above for parallel-flow. For a counter-flow shell and tube heat exchanger the effectiveness in equation (15) is replaced by

$$\epsilon = \frac{1-e^{-NTU(1-c)}}{1-ce^{-NTU(1-c)}}$$

Chapter 9   Ball Valve

Objectives

- Creating the SolidWorks parts and assembly for the ball valve, housing and pipe section
- Setting up Flow Simulation projects for internal flow
- Creating lids for the assembly
- Inserting boundary conditions
- Creating surface goals
- Running the calculations
- Using cut plots to visualize the resulting flow field
- Determine hydraulic resistance for the ball valve

Problem Description

SolidWorks Flow Simulation will be used to study the flow through a ball valve. The pipe has an inner diameter of 50 mm and the length of the pipe is 600 mm on each side of the ball valve. Air will be used as the fluid and the inlet velocity will be set to 10 m/s. The velocity and the pressure distribution at the ball valve will be shown and the hydraulic resistance of the valve will be determined for an opening angle of 20 degrees.

Figure 9.0 SolidWorks assembly for ball valve, housing and pipe section

Creating the Ball Valve

1. Start by creating a new part in SolidWorks: select **File>>New** and click on the **OK** button in the **New SolidWorks Document** window. Click on **Front Plane** in the **FeatureManager design tree** and select **Front** from the **View Orientation** drop down menu in the graphics window.

Figure 9.1a) Selection of front plane

Figure 9.1b) Selection of front view

2. Click on **Centerline** from the **Sketch** tools tab. Draw a 70.00 mm long vertical centerline through the origin. Close the **Line Properties** dialog box by clicking on ✔ .

Figure 9.2a) Selecting the centerline sketch tool

Figure 9.2b) Vertical centerline

3. Select **Centerpoint Arc** from the **Sketch** tools. Click at the origin in the graphics window, then click somewhere on the vertical center line above the origin and complete the half-circle by finally clicking on the vertical center line below the origin. Fill in the **Parameters** for the half-circle as shown in figure 9.3b). Close the ⬠ **Arc** dialog box by clicking on ✔ .

Figure 9.3a) Selecting the center point arc sketch tool

Figure 9.3b) Sketch of a half-circle

4. Select the **Features** tab and the **Revolved Boss/Base**, see figure 9.4a). Answer yes to the question if you want the sketch to be automatically closed. Close the **Revolve** dialog box by clicking on

OK ✓ . Right click in the graphics window and select **Zoom/Pan/Rotate>>Zoom to Fit**. Select **Front** view from **View Orientation** in the graphics window, see figure 9.1b). Select **Top Plane** from **Featuremanager design tree**. Insert a new plane from the SolidWorks menu by selecting **Insert>>Reference Geometry>>Plane**. Set the **Offset Distance** to **25.00mm** and exit the **Plane** dialog box. Select **Top** view from **View Orientation** in the graphics window, see figure 9.4e).

Figure 9.4a) Revolved boss/base feature

Figure 9.4b) Selecting top plane

Figure 9.4c) Inserting a plane

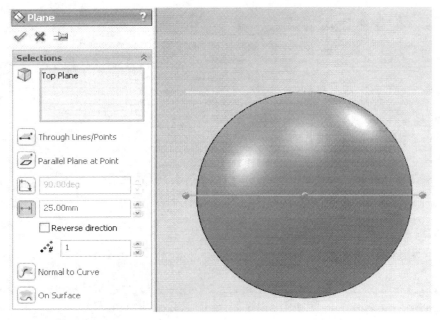

Figure 9.4d) Setting the location of the plane

Figure 9.4e) Selecting a top view

5. Click on **Plane 1** in the **Featuremanager design tree** and select **Circle** from the **Sketch** tools. Draw a circle with the parameters as given in figure 9.5a). Close the **Circle** dialog box by clicking on **OK** . Select the **Features** tab and **Extruded Boss/Base**. Set the **Depth** of the extrusion to **50.00mm**. Check the **Direction 2** box and select **Up To Next** from the drop down menu. Close the **Extrude** dialog box by clicking on **OK** .

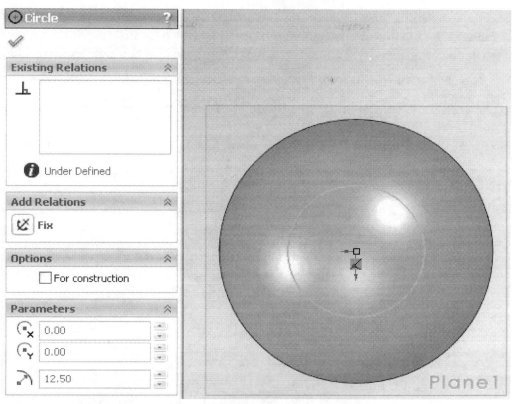

Figure 9.5a) Drawing of a circle for the extrusion

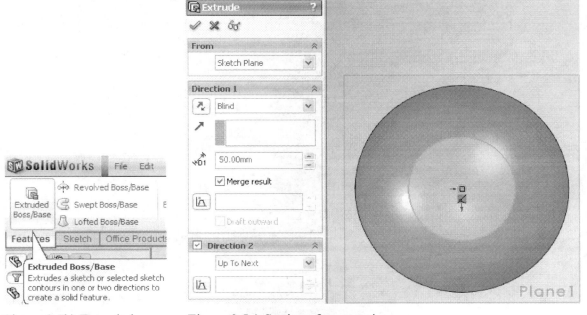

Figure 9.5b) Extruded
boss/base

Figure 9.5c) Settings for extrusion

6. Select **Front** view from **View Orientation** in the graphics window, see figure 9.1b). Click on **Front Plane** in the **Featuremanager design tree** and select **Circle** from the **Sketch** tools. Draw a circle with the parameters as given in figure 9.6a). Close the **Circle** dialog box by clicking on **OK** ✓ . Select **Extruded Cut** from **Features** tab. Select **Through All** from the drop-down menu for both directions, see figure 9.6c). Close the **Extrude** dialog box by clicking on **OK** ✓ .

Figure 9.6a) Settings for dimensions of a circle

Figure 9.6b) Selection of extruded cut

Figure 9.6c) Settings for extruded cut

7. Click on **Front Plane** in the **Featuremanager design tree** and select **Corner Rectangle** from the **Sketch** tools. Draw a rectangle with the parameters as given in figure 9.7b). Close the **Rectangle** dialog box by clicking on **OK** ✔. Select the **Features** tab and **Extruded Boss/Base**. Set the **Depth** of the extrusion to **30.00mm** in both directions. Close the **Extrude** dialog box by clicking on **OK** ✔. Save the part with the name "**Ball Valve**".

Figure 9.7a) Selection of corner rectangle   Figure 9.7b) Parameter settings for rectangle

Figure 9.7c) Directions setting for extrusion

Creating the Ball Valve Housing and Pipe Sections

8. Create another part in SolidWorks: select **File>>New** and click on the **OK** button in the **New SolidWorks Document** window. Click on **Front Plane** in the **FeatureManager design tree** and select **Front** from the **View Orientation** drop down menu in the graphics window, see step 1.

Repeat step 2 by selecting the **Centerline** from the **Sketch** tools tab. Draw a 70.00 mm long vertical centerline through the origin. Close the **Line Properties** dialog box and the **Insert Line** dialog by clicking on ✓ .

Select **Centerpoint Arc** from the **Sketch** tools. Click at the origin in the graphics window, then click somewhere on the vertical center line below the origin and complete the arc at an angle of 150°. Set the angle to 150.00° and fill in the other **Parameters** for the arc section as shown in figure 9.8a). Close the ⌂ **Arc** dialog box by clicking on ✓ . Repeat this process and create another arc section, see figure 9.8b). Next, use the **Line Sketch** tool and complete the closed contour as shown in figure 9.8c). Start by completing the vertical line on the centerline. Next, draw the inner vertical line with a length of 20 mm, see figure 9.8c). Continue with the short horizontal line and close the contour with the outer vertical line. Close the **Line Properties** dialog box and the **Insert Line** dialog by clicking on ✓ .

Figure 9.8a) Parameters for first arc section   Figure 9.8b) Parameters for second arc section

Figure 9.8c) Completed closed contour

9. Select the **Features** tab and the **Revolved Boss/Base**. Click on the vertical center line in the graphics window. Close the **Revolve** dialog box by clicking on **OK** ✓. Right click in the graphics window and select **Zoom/Pan/Rotate>>Zoom to Fit**. Select **Front** view from **View Orientation** in the graphics window, see figure 9.1b).

Figure 9.9 Housing for the ball valve

10. Click on **Front Plane** in the **Featuremanager design tree** and select **Circle** from the **Sketch** tools. Draw a circle with **15 mm** radius, see figure 9.10a). Close the **Circle** dialog box by clicking on **OK** ✓. Select **Extruded Cut** from **Features** tab. Select **Through All** from the drop-down menu for both directions. Close the **Extrude** dialog box by clicking on **OK** ✓.

Figure 9.10a) Dimensions of the circle   Figure 9.10b) Extrusion of ball valve housing

11. Select **Front Plane** from **Featuremanager design tree**. Insert a new plane from the SolidWorks menu by selecting **Insert>>Reference Geometry>>Plane**. Set the **Offset Distance** to **30.00mm** and exit the **Plane** dialog box. Click on **Plane 1** in the **Featuremanager design tree** and select **Circle** from the **Sketch** tools. Draw a circle with a radius of **15.00mm**. Close the **Circle** dialog box by clicking on **OK** ✓. Select the **Features** tab and **Extruded Boss/Base**. Set the **Depth D1** of the extrusion in **Direction 1** to **600.00mm**. Check the **Direction 2** box and select **Up To Next**

from the drop down menu. Check the **Thin Feature** box and set the thickness **T1** to **5.00mm**. Close the **Extrude** dialog box by clicking on **OK** ✓ .

Figure 9.11a) Setting the location of the new plane

Figure 11b) Drawing of a circle

Figure 9.11c) Settings for the pipe extrusion

12. Repeat step 11 by selecting **Front Plane** from **Featuremanager design tree**. Insert a new plane from the SolidWorks menu by selecting **Insert>>Reference Geometry>>Plane**. Set the **Offset Distance** to **30.00mm** and check the **Reverse direction** box and exit the **Plane** dialog box. Click on **Plane 2** in the **Featuremanager design tree** and select **Circle** from the **Sketch** tools. Draw a circle with a radius of **15.00mm**. Close the **Circle** dialog box by clicking on **OK** ✓ . Select the **Features** tab and **Extruded Boss/Base**. Click on the ⬚ **Reverse Direction** button for

Direction 1. Check the **Thin Feature** box and set the thickness **T1** to **5.00mm**. Check the **Direction 2** box and select **Up To Next** from the drop down menu. Close the **Extrude** dialog box by clicking on **OK** .

Figure 9.12a) Settings for the location of plane   Figure 9.12b) Settings for the pipe extrusion

13. Select **Left** view from **View Orientation** in the graphics window. Right click in the graphics window and select **Zoom/Pan/Rotate>>Zoom to Fit**. Save the part with the name "**Ball Valve Housing and Pipe Sections**".

Figure 9.13 Finished ball valve housing and pipe sections

Creating the Ball Valve and Pipe Assembly

14. Create a new assembly in SolidWorks: select **File>>New** and click on the **Assembly** button followed by the **OK** button in the **New SolidWorks Document** window. Click on **Front Plane** in the **FeatureManager design tree** and select **Front** from the **View Orientation** drop down menu in the graphics window. Select the **Browse...** button in the **Begin Assembly** window and open the **Ball Valve Housing and Pipe Sections** part. Click in the graphics window. Select **Isometric** view from **View Orientation** in the graphics window. Select **Insert>>Component>>Existing Part/Assembly...** from the SolidWorks menu. Select the **Browse...** button in the **Insert Component** window and open the **Ball Valve** part. Click in the graphics window above the other part. Select **Insert>>Mate...** from the SolidWorks menu. Click on the cylindrical face of the ball valve and the inner cylindrical face of the ball valve housing. Select the **Concentric** standard mate and exit the **Concentric 1** window. Exit the **Mate** window.

Figure 9.14a) Creating a new assembly   Figure 9.14b) Inserting an existing part

Figure 9.14c) Inserting a mate   Figure 9.14d) Creating a concentric mate

15. Select **Insert>>Mate…** from the SolidWorks menu. Right click in the **Mate Selections** portion of the **Mate** window and select **Clear Selections**. Select the spherical face of the ball valve and the inner spherical face of the ball valve housing by right clicking on the outer face of the housing and selecting **Select Other**, see figure 9.15a). Select the inner spherical face of the housing and exit the **Concentric2** window. Exit the **Mate** window. You should now have figure 9.15b) in your graphics window.

Figure 9.15a) Selecting the valve housing

Figure 9.15b) Ball valve and housing

16. Select **Insert>>Mate...** from the SolidWorks menu. Select the **Front Plane** from the ball valve housing on the fly-out assembly and also select the corresponding **Front Plane** from the ball valve. Select the ⬚ **Angle** button from **Standard Mates** and enter **20.00 deg**. Exit both the angle window and the mate window.

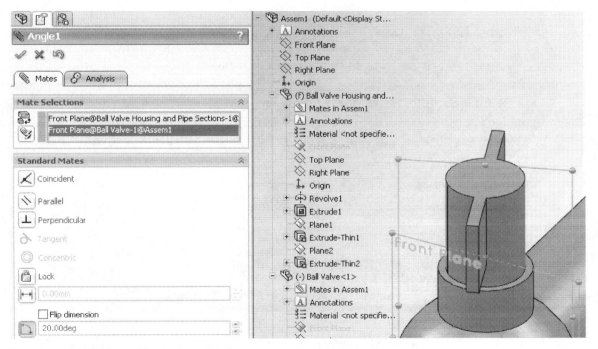

Figure 9.16) Settings for angle mate

17. Select **Front** view from **View Orientation** in the graphics window. You have now finished the ball valve assembly and in figure 9.17 you can see the partially open ball valve. Save the assembly with the name "**Ball Valve and Pipe Assembly**".

Figure 9.17 Ball valve assembly with partially open valve

Setting up the Flow Simulation Project for the Ball Valve

18. If Flow Simulation is not available in the menu, you have to add it from SolidWorks menu: **Tools>>Add Ins...** and check the corresponding **SolidWorks Flow Simulation** box. Select **Flow Simulation>>Project>>Wizard** to create a new Flow Simulation project. Create a new figuration named "**Ball Valve Study**". Click on the **Next >** button. Select the default **SI (m-kg-s)** unit system and click on the **Next>** button once again. Use the default **Internal Analysis type**. Click on the **Next >** button.

Figure 9.18a) Starting a new Flow Simulation project

Figure 9.18b) Creating a name for the project

19. Add **Air** from **Gases** as the **Project Fluid**. Click on the **Next >** button. Use the default **Wall Conditions**. Click on the **Next >** button. Use the default **Initial Conditions**. Click on the **Next >** button. Set the **Result resolution** to **6**. Click on the **Finish** button.

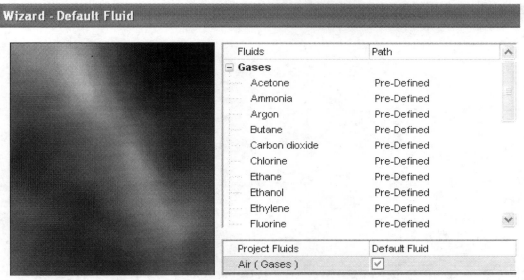

Figure 9.19a) Adding air as the project fluid

Figure 9.19b) Setting result resolution

Creating Lids and Setting the Minimum Gap Size and Number of Cells

20. Select **Flow Simulation>>Tools>>Create Lids…** from the SolidWorks menu. Select **Front** view from **View Orientation** in the graphics window. Select the face as shown in figure 9.20b).

Close the **Create Lids** dialog box by clicking on **OK** ✓ . Answer yes to the question if you want to reset mesh setting. Select **Flow Simulation>>Tools>>Create Lids…** from the SolidWorks menu. Select **Back** view from **View Orientation** in the graphics window. Select the similar face as above and close the **Create Lids** dialog box by clicking on **OK** ✓ . Answer yes to the questions if you want to reset the computational domain and the mesh setting.

Figure 9.20a) Creating a lid

Figure 9.20b) Selection of surface for lid

Select **Flow Simulation>>Initial Mesh....** Check the box for **Manual specification of the minimum gap size**. Enter the value **0.022255 m** for **Minimum gap size**. This is the size d of the opening as shown in figure 9.17 for a valve angle of 20 degrees. The size of the opening can be determined from the valve angle θ, the closed valve angle $\theta_c = 73.74°$ and the diameter of the ball $D_b = 50\ mm$.

$$d = \sqrt{D_b^2 Sin^2\left(\frac{\theta_c - \theta}{2}\right) - \frac{D_b^2}{4}\left(Cos\left(\frac{\theta_c}{2} - \theta\right) - Cos\left(\frac{\theta_c}{2}\right)\right)^2} \qquad (1)$$

where $\theta_c = 2Sin^{-1}(D_p/D_b)$ and $D_p = 30$ mm is the inner diameter of the pipe section.

Uncheck the box for **Automatic settings** at the bottom of the **Initial Mesh** window. Set the **Number of cells per X:** to **8**, the **Number of cells per Y:** to **6** and the **Number of cells per Z:** to **236**.

Inserting Boundary Conditions

21. Select **Left** view from **View Orientation** in the graphics window. Right-click in the graphics window and select **Zoom/Pan/Rotate>>Zoom to Area**. Zoom in on the left end of the pipe, right click in the graphics window and select **Zoom/Pan/Rotate>>Rotate View**. Rotate the view a little bit, see figure 9.21. Click on the plus sign next to the **Input Data** folder in the **Flow Simulation analysis tree**. Right click on 🗔 **Boundary Conditions** and select **Insert Boundary Condition....** Right click on the end section of the pipe and select **Select Other**. Select the inner surface of the lid, see figure 9.21. Select **Inlet Velocity** in the **Type** portion of the boundary condition window. Set the inlet velocity to **10 m/s**. Click OK ✔ to exit the **Boundary Condition** window.

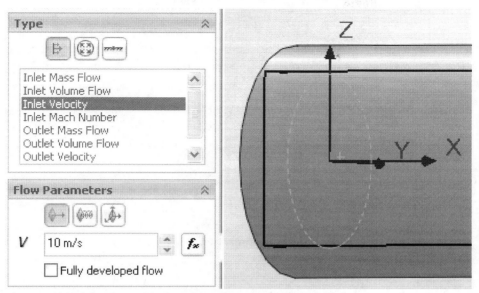

Figure 9.21 Selection of inflow boundary condition

22. Select **Left** view from **View Orientation** in the graphics window. Select **Zoom/Pan/Rotate>>Zoom to Area** and zoom in on the right end of the pipe, right click in the graphics window and select **Zoom/Pan/Rotate>>Rotate View**. Rotate the view a little bit. Right click on **Boundary Conditions** and select **Insert Boundary Condition….** Right click on the pipe and select the inner surface of the pipe outflow lid, see figure 9.22. Select **Pressure Openings** in the **Type** portion of the **Boundary Condition** window. Select **Static Pressure**. Click OK to exit the **Boundary Condition** window.

Figure 9.22 Selection of outflow boundary condition

Inserting Goals

23. Right click on **Goals** in the **Flow Simulation analysis tree** and select **Insert Surface Goals....** Click on the **Flow Simulation analysis tree** tab and select the **Inlet Velocity 1** boundary condition. Select **Average Total Pressure** as a surface goal for the inner surface of the inflow lid. Click OK ✓ to exit the **Surface Goals** window. Repeat this step and select the **Static Pressure 1** boundary condition and insert an average total pressure surface goal for the inner surface of the outflow lid.

Figure 9.23 Selection of surface goal

Running the Calculations for Ball Valve

24. Select **Flow Simulation>> Calculation Control Options...** from the SolidWorks menu, click on the **Refinement** tab and disable the refinement from the **Value** drop down menu. Click on the **OK** button to exit the window. Select **Flow Simulation>>Solve>>Run** to start calculations. Click on the **Run** button in the **Run** window.

Figure 9.24a) Starting calculations   Figure 9.24b) Run window

Figure 9.24c) Solver window, valve angle θ = 20 deg

Inserting Cut Plots

25. Right click on **Cut Plots** in the **Flow Simulation analysis tree** and select **Insert…**. Select the **Top Plane** from the **FeatureManager design tree** for the **Ball Valve and Pipe Assembly**. Click on the **Vectors** button in the **Display** portion of the **Cut Plot** window. Click on ⌈ View Settings... ⌋. Slide the **Number of colors:** slide bar to **101**. Select **Velocity** from the **Parameter:** dropdown menu. Click on ⌈ OK ⌋. Click OK ✔ to exit the **Cut Plot** window. Rename the cut plot to **Velocity for valve angle = 20 deg**. Click on the **Flow Simulation** tab and the **Geometry** button to display the cut plot. Also, click on the **Lightning** button located above the geometry button. Select **Top** view from **View Orientation** in the graphics window. We see the velocity distribution in figure 9.25b). Repeat this step but select **Pressure** instead of **Velocity**, see figure 9.25c). Click on this button for both min and max pressure to display a broader spectrum of colors for the cut plot. Rename the cut plot to **Pressure for valve angle = 20 deg**.

Figure 9.25a) Geometry button in Flow Simulation

Figure 9.25b) Ball valve velocity distribution   Figure 9.25c) Ball valve pressure distribution

Determining Hydraulic Resistance

26. In the next step we want to determine the hydraulic resistance of the ball valve. In order to do this, we first have to determine the total pressure drop without the valve. Click on the plus sign next to **Mates** in the **Featuremanager Design Tree**. Right click on **Angle1** and select **Edit Feature** and set the angle θ to **0.00deg**. Exit the **Angle1** and **Mate** windows. Answer yes to the question if you want to reset the computational domain. Select **Flow Simulation>>Initial Mesh…**. Check the box for **Automatic settings** at the bottom of the **Initial Mesh** window. Check the box for **Manual specification of the minimum gap size**. Enter the value **0.03 m** for **Minimum gap size**. This value is the inside diameter of the pipe. Select **Flow Simulation>>Initial Mesh…** and uncheck the **Automatic settings** box. Set the **Number of cells per X** to **6**, **Number of cells per Y** to **6** and **Number of cells per Z** to **240**. Click on the **OK** button to exit.

Select **Flow Simulation>>Solve>>Run** to start calculations. Click on the **Run** button in the **Run** window. Repeat step 25 and create a cut plot with the velocity distribution for the ball valve for zero valve angle θ, see figure 9.26c).

Figure 9.26a) Changing the angle of the ball valve

Figure 9.26b) Solver window, valve angle $\theta = 0$ deg

From Figure 9.26b) in the list of goals, we see that the total pressure difference between inlet and outlet based on average values is 101,448 Pa – 101,385 Pa = 63 Pa. This value has to be subtracted from the difference value that we determine from figure 9.24c). The final total pressure difference over the valve is 76 Pa for a 20 deg valve angle. We can now determine the hydraulic resistance ξ of the valve to be

$$\xi = \frac{2\Delta P}{\rho U^2} = \frac{2 \cdot 76 \text{Pa}}{1.204 \frac{kg}{m^3} \cdot 10^2 m^2/s^2} = 1.26 \tag{2}$$

where ρ is the density of air, ΔP is the difference in total pressure over the valve and U is the average velocity in the pipe.

Figure 9.26c) Ball valve velocity distribution for zero valve angle

References

[1] Idelchik, I.E., Handbook for Hydraulic Resistance, Jaico Publishing House, 2005.

[2] SolidWorks Flow Simulation 2009 Tutorial

Exercises

1. Change the mesh resolution in the FlowWorks simulations and study how the mesh size affects the velocity and pressure distributions and the hydraulic resistance.

2. Set the angle θ of the ball valve to different values and compare the results with those shown in this chapter. Determine and plot the variation in hydraulic resistance with ball valve angle.

Notes:

Chapter 10   Orifice Plate and Flow Nozzle

Objectives

- Creating the SolidWorks part for the orifice plate
- Setting up Flow Simulation projects for internal flow
- Inserting boundary conditions
- Creating point goals
- Running the calculations
- Using cut plots, XY plots and flow trajectories to visualize the resulting flow fields
- Determine discharge coefficients for orifice plate and flow nozzle

Problem Description

We will use Flow Simulation to study the flow through an orifice plate and a long radius flow nozzle. Obstruction flow meters are commonly in use to measure flow rates in pipes. Both the orifice and nozzle are modeled inside a pipe with an inner diameter of 50 mm and a length of 1 m. Water in the pipe flows with a mean velocity of 1 m/s corresponding to a Reynolds number Re = 50,000. The opening in the orifice is 20 mm in diameter. The long radius nozzle has a length of 33.6 mm and the opening is 21 mm in diameter. We will study how the centerline velocity varies along the length of the pipe for both cases and plot both pressure and velocity fields. The discharge coefficients will be determined and compared with experimental values.

Figure 10.0a) SolidWorks model of orifice plate

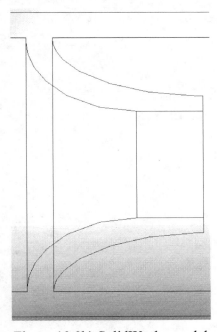

Figure 10.0b) SolidWorks model of nozzle

Creating the Orifice Plate in a Pipe

1. Start by creating a new part in SolidWorks: select **File>>New**, select **Part** and click on the **OK** button in the **New SolidWorks Document** window. Click on **Front Plane** in the **FeatureManager design tree** and select **Front** from the **View Orientation** drop down menu in the graphics window.

Figure 10.1a) Selection of front plane   Figure 10.1b) Selection of front view

2. Click on **Circle** from the **Sketch** tools tab. Draw a circle with a **25.00mm** radius. Close the **Circle** dialog box by clicking on .

Figure 10.2a) Selecting the circle sketch tool

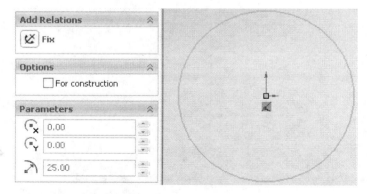

Figure 10.2b) Sketch of a circle

3. Select the **Features** tab and **Extruded Boss/Base**. Set the **Depth** of the extrusion to **500.00mm** in both directions. Check the **Thin Feature** box and enter a **Thickness** value of **5.00mm**. Check the **Cap ends** box and enter **5.00 mm** for the thickness. Close the **Extrude** dialog box by clicking on **OK** ✓.

Figure 10.3a) Selecting extruded boss/base feature

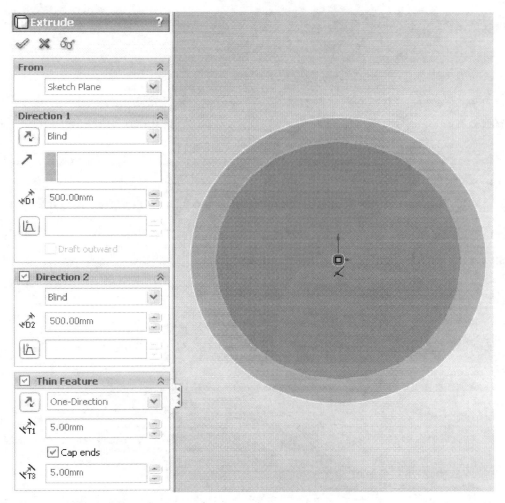

Figure 10.3b) Settings for extrusion

4. Select **Front** view from **View Orientation** in the graphics window. Click on **Front Plane** in the **Featuremanager design tree** and select **Circle** from the **Sketch** tools. Draw a circle with a **25 mm** radius, see figure 10.4a). Close the **Circle** dialog box by clicking on **OK** ✓ . Select the **Features** tab and **Extruded Boss/Base**. Set the **Depth** of the extrusion to **0.50mm** in both directions. Close the **Extrude** dialog box by clicking on **OK** ✓ .

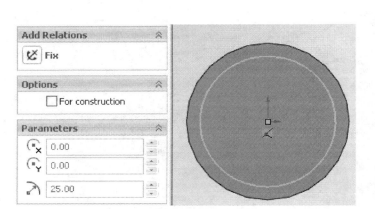

Figure 10.4a) Parameter settings for a circle   Figure 10.4b) Settings for extrusion

5. Click on **Front Plane** in the **Featuremanager design tree** and select **Circle** from the **Sketch** tools. Draw a circle with a **10 mm** radius, see figure 10.5a). Close the **Circle** dialog box by clicking on **OK** ✓ . Select the **Features** tab and **Extruded Cut**. Set the **Depth** of the cut to **0.50mm** in both directions. Click on the **Draft** button for **Direction 2** and enter **45.00deg**. Check the **Draft outward** box, see figure 10.5c). Exit ✓ the extrude window.

Figure 10.5a) Circle parameters   Figure 10.5b) Extruded cut feature

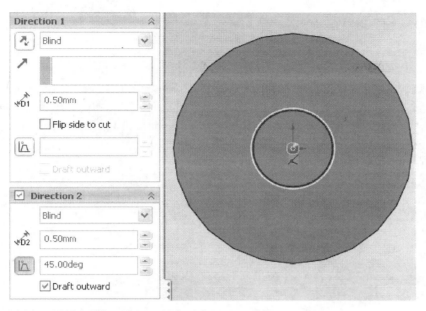

Figure 10.5c) Directions setting for extrusion

6. Select **Left** view from **View Orientation** in the graphics window. Select **Wireframe** display style from the drop down menu in the graphics window. Select **Zoom/Pan/Rotate>>Zoom to Area** and zoom in on the middle section of the pipe, right click in the graphics window and select **Zoom/Pan/Rotate>>Rotate View**. Rotate the view a little bit to get figure 10.6b). You have now completed your orifice plate inside a pipe. Save the part as **Orifice Plate**.

Figure 10.6a) Wireframe display style   Figure 10.6b) Orifice plate

Setting up the Flow Simulation Project for the Orifice Plate

7. If Flow Simulation is not available in the menu, you have to add it from SolidWorks menu: **Tools>>Add Ins…** and check the corresponding **SolidWorks Flow Simulation** box. Select **Flow Simulation>>Project>>Wizard** to create a new Flow Simulation project. Create a new figuration named "**Orifice Plate Study**". Click on the **Next >** button. Select the default **SI (m-kg-s)** unit system and click on the **Next>** button once again. Use the default **Internal Analysis type**. Click on the **Next >** button.

Figure 10.7a) Starting a new Flow Simulation project

Figure 10.7b) Creating a name for the project

8. Add **Water** from **Liquids** as the **Project Fluid**. Click on the **Next >** button. Use the default **Wall Conditions**. Click on the **Next >** button. Use the default **Initital Conditions**. Click on the **Next >** button. Set the **Result resolution** to **5**. Check the box **Manual specification of the minimum gap size** and set the **Minimum gap size:** to **0.02 m**. Check the box **Manual specification of the minimum wall thickness** and set **Minimum wall thickness:** to **0.001 m**. This is done in order to resolve the opening of the orifice and the thickness of the orifice plate. Click on the **Finish** button.

Figure 10.8a) Adding air as the project fluid

Figure 10.8b) Setting the result resolution, minimum gap size and minimum wall thickness

Inserting Boundary Conditions

9. Select **Left** view from **View Orientation** in the graphics window. Select
Zoom/Pan/Rotate>>Zoom to Area and zoom in on the left end of the pipe, right click in the
graphics window and select **Zoom/Pan/Rotate>>Rotate View**. Rotate the view a little bit, see
figure 10.9a). Click on the plus sign next to the **Input Data** folder in the **Flow Simulation**
analysis tree. Right click on **Computational Domain** and select **Hide**. Right click on
Boundary Conditions and select **Insert Boundary Condition…**. Right click on the end of the
pipe and select **Select Other**. Select the inner surface of the end cap. Select **Inlet Velocity** in the
Type portion of the boundary condition window. Set the inlet velocity to **1 m/s** and check the box
for **Fully developed flow**, see figure 10.9a). Click OK to exit the **Boundary Condition**
window. Red arrows will appear showing the inlet velocity boundary condition, see figure 10.9b)

Figure 10.9a) Selection of inflow boundary condition   Figure 10.9b) Inlet velocity

10. Select **Left** view from **View Orientation** in the graphics window. Select
Zoom/Pan/Rotate>>Zoom to Area and zoom in on the right end of the pipe, right click in the
graphics window and select **Zoom/Pan/Rotate>>Rotate View**. Rotate the view a little bit, see
figure 10.10a). Right click on 🗗 **Boundary Conditions** and select **Insert Boundary
Condition…**. Right click on the end of the pipe and select **Select Other**. Select the inner surface
of the pipe outflow cap. Select ⊛ **Pressure Openings** in the **Type** portion of the **Boundary
Condition** window. Select **Static Pressure**. Click OK ✓ to exit the **Boundary Condition**
window.

 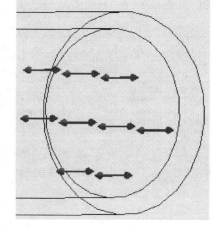

Figure 10.10a) Selection of outflow boundary condition   Figure 10.10b) Static pressure

Inserting Goals

11. Right click on **Goals** in the **Flow Simulation analysis tree** and select **Insert Point Goals….**. Click on the Point Coordinates button and enter the coordinates as shown in figure 10.11a).

    Check the **Static Pressure** box as a point goal for the coordinate. Click on the **Add Point** button to add this point to the table. Add another point to the table of point goals and make sure that the **Static Pressure** box is checked, see figure 10.11b). Click OK ✓ to exit the **Point Goals** window.

Figure 10.11a) Selection of first point   Figure 10.11b) Selection of second point

Running the Calculations for Orifice Plate

12. Select **Flow Simulation>>Solve>>Run** to start calculations. Click on the **Run** button in the **Run** window.

    Click on 🏁 **Insert Goals Table** to view the static pressure goals in a table. Click on 📉 **Insert Goals Plot** to view a graph of the pressure goals. Click on the **Add All** button in the **Add/Remove Goals** window and click on the **OK** button to exit the window.

Figure 10.12a) Starting calculations   Figure 10.12b) Run window

Figure 10.12c) Inserting goals table   Figure 10.12d) Inserting goals graph

Figure 10.12e) Adding goals to the goals plot

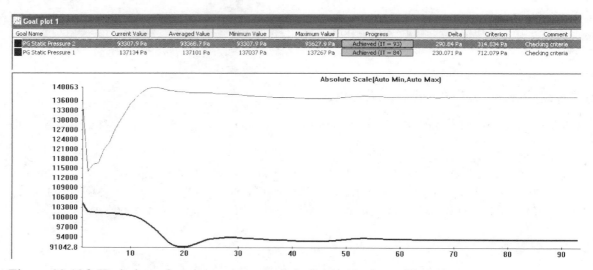

Figure 10.12f) Variation of static pressure goals before and after orifice plate

Figure 10.12g) Solver window for orifice plate flow

Inserting Cut Plots

13. Right click on **Cut Plots** in the **Flow Simulation analysis tree** and select **Insert…**. Select the **Right Plane** from the **FeatureManager design tree**. Click on **View Settings…**. Slide the **Number of colors:** slide bar to **101**. Select **Z-Velocity** from the **Parameter:** dropdown menu. Click on **OK**. Click OK to exit the **Cut Plot** window. Rename the cut plot to **Z-velocity**.

Click on the **Flow Simulation** tab and the **Lighting** button to apply lighting to the cut plot. Select **Left** view from **View Orientation** in the graphics window, see figure 10.13b). Repeat this step but this time click on **View Settings** and select **Pressure** from the **Parameter:** dropdown menu. Click on **OK**. Click OK to exit the **Cut Plot** window, see figure 10.13c). Rename the cut plot to **Pressure**.

Figure 10.13a) Lighting button in Flow Simulation

Figure 10.13b) Z-velocity distribution before and after the orifice plate

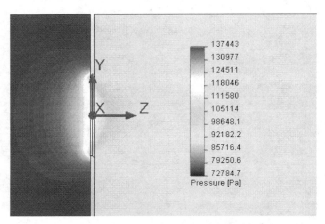

Figure 10.13c) Pressure distribution before and after the orifice plate

Determining Discharge Coefficient for Orifice Plate

14. From a mass balance and from Bernoulli equation we can derive an expression for the velocity at the orifice V_o

$$V_o = \sqrt{\frac{2\Delta P}{\rho(1-\beta^4)}} \tag{1}$$

where $\Delta P = P_1 - P_2$ is the pressure difference between the pressure P_1 before and P_2 after the orifice, ρ is the density of the fluid and $\beta = d/D$ is the ratio of the orifice diameter d and the inner pipe diameter D. Due to frictional effects and the vena contracta, we have to incorporate a correction factor known as the discharge coefficient C_d in order to determine the volume flow rate $\dot{V}$ in the pipe

$$\dot{V} = C_d A_o V_o \tag{2}$$

where A_o is the area of the orifice hole. The discharge coefficient has been experimentally determined for orifice flow meters as

$$C_d = 0.5959 + 0.0312\beta^{2.1} - 0.184\beta^8 + 91.71\frac{\beta^{2.5}}{Re^{0.75}} + 0.09A\frac{\beta^4}{1-\beta^4} - 0.0337B\beta^3 \qquad (3)$$

where the Reynolds number $Re = V_1D/\nu$ is based on the approach velocity V_1 and kinematic viscosity ν of the fluid. The constants A and B are zero for corner taps (pipe wall taps, one on each side adjacent to the orifice plate) that have the values $A = 0.4333$ and $B = 0.47$ for pipe wall taps located the distance D upstream from the orifice and $D/2$ downstream. Equation (3) is valid in the region $10^4 < Re < 10^7$, $0.25 < \beta < 0.75$.

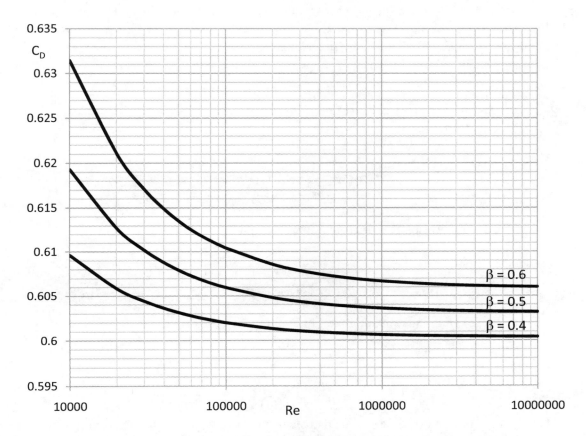

Figure 10.14a) Discharge coefficient versus Reynolds number for three different β ratios, pipe wall taps located distance D upstream and $D/2$ downstream from orifice plate

The diameter ratio $\beta = 20mm/50mm = 0.4$ in the Flow Simulation calculations and the Reynolds number is

$$Re = \frac{V_1 D}{\nu} = \frac{1m/s \cdot 0.050m}{1 \cdot 10^{-6}m^2/s} = 50,000 \qquad (4)$$

The pressure difference can be determined from data in figure 10.12g) as $\Delta P = 137{,}020\ Pa - 93{,}333.5 = 43{,}686.5\ Pa$. The discharge coefficient from Flow Simulation is

$$C_D = \frac{\dot{V}}{A_o V_o} = \frac{A_1 V_1}{A_o}\sqrt{\frac{\rho(1-\beta^4)}{2\Delta P}} = \frac{V_1}{\beta^2}\sqrt{\frac{\rho(1-\beta^4)}{2\Delta P}} = \frac{1 m/s}{0.4^2}\sqrt{\frac{998 kg/m^3(1-0.4^4)}{2\cdot43{,}686.5\ Pa}} = 0.659 \quad (5)$$

The corresponding value from experiments, equation (3), is 0.603, a 9 % difference.

We would now like to see the velocity and pressure variation along the pipe. Click on the **Featuremanager design tree** tab and select the **Right Plane**. Select **Line** from the **Sketch** tools. Draw a horizontal **990.00 mm** long line along the pipe wall, see figure 10.14b). Exit the **Line Properties** window and the **Insert Line** window. Rename the sketch and call it "**Wall**". Click on

Rebuild from the SolidWorks menu. Repeat this step and sketch another horizontal line with the same length along the centerline of the pipe, see figure 10.14c) and name the sketch "**Centerline**".

Figure 10.14b) Drawing of a horizontal lines along the pipe wall

Figure 10.14c) Drawing of a horizontal lines along the pipe centerline

Inserting XY Plots

Click on the **Flow Simulation analysis tree** tab and right click on **XY Plots** and select **Insert…**. Click on the **Featuremanager design tree** tab and select the sketch named "**Centerline**". Choose **Model Z** from the **Abscissa:** drop down menu. Check the **Velocity** box in the **Parameters** portion of the **XY Plot** window. Slide the **Resolution** to the maximum value and set the number of evenly distributed output points to **200**. Open the **Options** portion of the **XY Plot** window and select the template xy-plots.xlt, see figure 10.14d). Exit the **XY Plot**. An Excel file will open. The maximum velocity along the centerline is around eight times higher than the approach velocity, see figure 10.14e). Rename the XY Plot to in the Flow Simulation analysis tree to **Velocity along Centerline**. Repeat this step but select the sketch named "**Wall**" and check the box for **Pressure**. Rename the XY Plot to **Pressure along Wall**. We can see in figure 10.14f) that there is a partial recovery in pressure after the orifice.

Figure 10.14d) Settings for XY plot

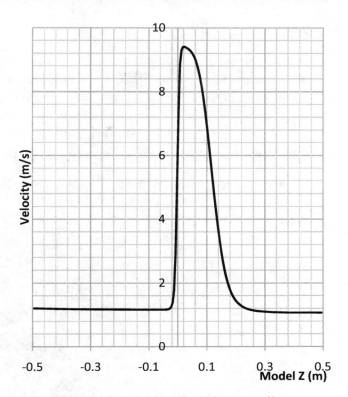

Figure 10.14e) Velocity along the centerline

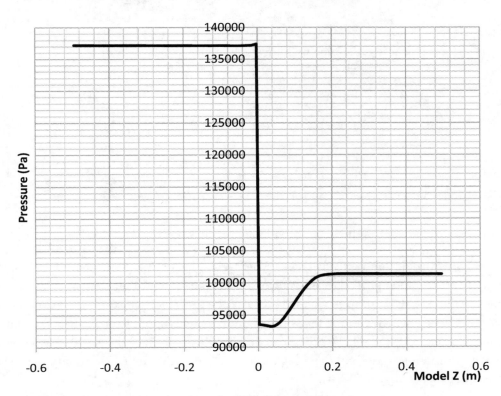

Figure 10.14f) Pressure variation along the pipe wall

Creating Sketch for XY Plots

Next, we want to see the variation of the velocity profile at different positions upstream and downstream of the orifice. Click on the **Featuremanager design tree** tab and select the **Right Plane**. Select **Line** from the **Sketch** tools. Draw vertical lines across the pipe at different model positions Z = -50, 50, 100, 150, 200mm. These positions are corresponding to x = 50, -50, -100, -150, and -200mm, see figure 10.14g) for the first vertical line at Z = -50mm (x = 50mm). Exit the **Line Properties** window when you have completed all five vertical lines, see figure 10.14h).

Name the sketch "**Velocity profiles**". Click on 🔧 **Rebuild** from the SolidWorks menu.

Figure 10.14g) First line across the pipe with local parameter values

Figure 10.14h) Five lines across the pipe for velocity profiles

Click on the **Flow Simulation analysis tree** tab and right click on **XY Plots** and select **Insert…**. Click on the **Featuremanager design tree** tab and select the sketch "**Velocity profiles**". Choose **Model Y** from the **Abscissa:** drop down menu. Check the **Z-Velocity** box in the **Parameters** portion of the **XY Plot** window. Slide the **Resolution** to the maximum value and set the number of evenly distributed output points to **200**. Open the **Options** portion of the **XY Plot** window and select the template xy-plots.xlt. Exit the **XY Plot**. Rename the XY Plot to **Z-velocity Profiles**. An Excel file will open, see figure 10.14i).

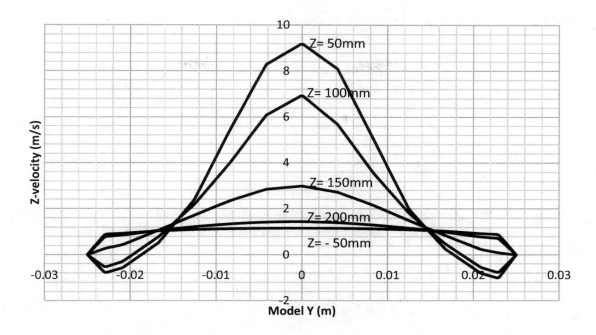

Figure 10.14i) Velocity profiles at different streamwise positions, results obtained for initial mesh level 5 and refinement of the mesh is disabled

Flow Trajectories

Flow trajectories show the streamlines of the flow and we will now insert them for the orifice plate flow. Right click on the **Pressure** cut plot in the Flow Simulation analysis tree and select **Hide**. Right click on the **Z-velocity** cut plot in the Flow Simulation analysis tree and select **Hide**. Right click on **Flow Trajectories** in the Flow Simulation analysis tree and select **Insert…**. Go to the FeatureManager design tree and click on the **Front Plane**. The front plane will now be listed as the **Reference:** plane in the **Flow Trajectories** window. Set the **Number of trajectories:** to **100**. Click on the **View Settings…** button and select **Velocity** from the **Parameter:** drop down menu. Click on the **OK** button to exit the **View Settings** window. Click on the **OK** button to exit the **Flow Trajectories** window.

Figure 10.14j) Flow trajectories for orifice plate flow

Running the Calculations for Long Radius Nozzle

15. Next, we will study the long radius flow nozzle meter. Open the file "**Long Radius Nozzle**". Select **Flow Simulation>>Solve>>Run…**. Check the **Mesh** box in the **Run** window and also check **New calculation** in the same window. Click on the **Run** button. Insert cut plots of Z-velocity and pressure in the same way as was shown in step 13. The cut plots for the long radius nozzle are shown in figures 10.15b) and 10.15c). Insert an XY-Plot of centerline velocity as was shown in step **14**, see figure 10.15e) for the result. Also, copy plot data and include centerline velocity for the orifice plate in the same graph. We see that the maximum velocity is 70 % higher for the orifice plate as compared with the long radius nozzle.

Figure 10.15a) Solver window for long radius nozzle calculation

Figure 10.15b) Z-velocity distribution along long-radius flow nozzle

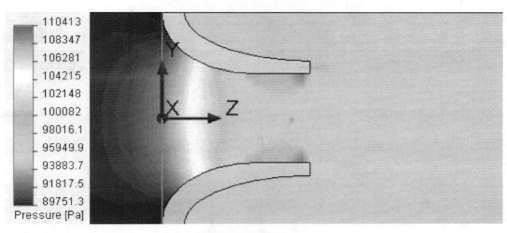

Figure 10.15c) Pressure distribution along long-radius flow nozzle

Determining Discharge Coefficient for Long Radius Nozzle

The discharge coefficient for the long radius nozzle is given by

$$C_d = 0.9975 - 6.53\sqrt{\frac{\beta}{Re}} \qquad (6)$$

Figure 10.15d) Discharge coefficient versus Reynolds number for three different β ratios

The diameter ratio $\beta = 21mm/50mm = 0.42$ in the Flow Simulation calculations and the Reynolds Re number is 50,000, see equation (4). The pressure difference can be determined from data in figure 10.15a) as $\Delta P = 110,016\ Pa - 97,443.1 = 12,572.9\ Pa$. The discharge coefficient from Flow Simulation is

$$C_D = \frac{\dot{V}}{A_o V_o} = \frac{A_1 V_1}{A_o}\sqrt{\frac{\rho(1-\beta^4)}{2\Delta P}} = \frac{V_1}{\beta^2}\sqrt{\frac{\rho(1-\beta^4)}{2\Delta P}} = \frac{1m/s}{0.42^2}\sqrt{\frac{998kg/m^3(1-0.42^4)}{2\cdot12,572.9\ \text{Pa}}} = 1.112 \qquad (7)$$

The corresponding value from experiments, equation (6), is 0.979, a 13.5 % difference.

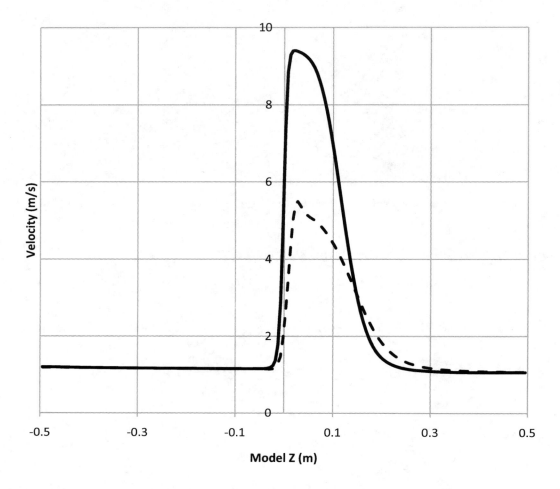

Figure 10.15e) A comparison of centerline velocity for orifice flow $\beta = 0.4$ (full line) and long-radius flow nozzle $\beta = 0.42$ (dashed line) at $Re = 50,000$

Reference

[1] White, F. M., Fluid Mechanics, 4th Edition, McGraw-Hill, 1999.

Exercises

1. Change the mesh resolution in flow simulations and see how the mesh size affects the discharge coefficient in comparison with experimental values for the orifice plate and long radius nozzle.

2. Determine the pressure difference between corner taps (where the orifice plate meets the pipe wall), determine the discharge coefficient using equation (5), and compare with equation (3) using values for $A = B = 0$.

3. Determine the discharge coefficient for different Reynolds numbers and compare with figure 10.14a) for the orifice plate and figure 10.15d) for the long-radius nozzle.

4. Keep the Reynolds number constant and determine the discharge coefficient for different β ratios and compare with figure 10.14a) for the orifice plate and figure 10.15d) for the long-radius nozzle.

Notes:

Chapter 11   Thermal Boundary Layer

Objectives

- Setting up Flow Simulation projects for internal flow
- Inserting boundary conditions, creating goals and running the calculations
- Using cut plots and XY plots to visualize the resulting flow field
- Compare Flow Simulation results with theoretical and empirical data

Problem Description

In this chapter, we will use Flow Simulation to study the thermal two-dimensional laminar and turbulent boundary layer flow on a flat plate and compare with the theoretical boundary layer solution and empirical results. The inlet velocity for the 1 m long plate is 5 m/s and we will be using air as the fluid for laminar calculations and water to get a higher Reynolds number for turbulent boundary layer calculations. The temperature of the hot wall will be set to 393.2 K while the temperature of the approaching free stream is set to 293.2 K. We will determine the temperature profiles and plot the same profiles using the well known boundary layer similarity coordinate. The variation of the local Nusselt number will also be determined.

Figure 11.0 Thermal velocity boundary layer close to horizontal wall

Setting up the Flow Simulation Project

1. Open the part named "**Thermal Boundary Layer Part 2009**".

Figure 11.1 SolidWorks model for thermal boundary layer

2. If Flow Simulation is not available in the menu, you have to add it from SolidWorks menu: **Tools>>Add Ins...** and check the corresponding **Flow Simulation** box. Select **Flow Simulation>>Project>>Wizard** to create a new Flow Simulation project. Create a new figuration named "**Thermal Boundary Layer Study**". Click on the **Next >** button. Select the default **SI (m-kg-s)** unit system and click on the **Next>** button once again.

Figure 11.2a) Starting a new Flow Simulation project

Figure 11.2b) Creating a name for the project

3. Use the default **Internal Analysis type**. Click on the **Next >** button.

Figure 11.3 Analysis type window

4. Select **Air** from the **Gases** and add it as **Project Fluid**. Select **Laminar Only** from the **Flow Type** drop down menu. Click on the **Next >** button. Use the default **Wall Conditions** and **5 m/s** for **Velocity in X direction** as **Initial Condition**. Slide the **Result resolution** to **8**. Click on the **Finish** button.

Figure 11.4 Selection of fluid for the project and flow type

5. Select **Flow Simulation>>Computational Domain...**. Click on the **Boundary Condition** tab and select **XY-Plane Flow** from the drop down menu. Click on the **OK** button to exit the **Computational Domain** window.

Figure 11.5a) Modifying the computational domain

Figure 11.5b) Selecting two dimensional flow condition

6. Select **Flow Simulation>>Initial Mesh...**. Uncheck the **Automatic setting** box at the bottom of the window. Change both the **Number of cells per X:** to **300** and the **Number of cells per Y:** to **200**. Click on the **OK** button to exit the **Initial Mesh** window.

Figure 11.6a) Modifying the initial mesh

Figure 11.6b) Changing the number of cells in both directions

Inserting Boundary Conditions

7. Select the **Flow Simulation analysis tree** tab, open the **Input Data** folder by clicking on the plus sign next to it and right click on **Boundary Conditions**. Select **Insert Boundary Condition….** Right click in the graphics window and select **Zoom/Pan/Rotate>>Rotate View**. Click and drag the mouse so that the inner surface of the left boundary is visible. Right click again and choose **Rotate View.** Click on the left inflow boundary surface. Select **Inlet Velocity** in the **Type** portion of the **Boundary Condition** window and set the velocity to **5 m/s** in the **Flow Parameters** window. Click **OK** ✔ to exit the window. Right click in the graphics window and select **Zoom/Pan/Rotate>>** 🔍 **Zoom to Area** and select an area around the left boundary.

Figure 11.7a) Inserting boundary condition   Figure 11.7b) Modifying the view

Figure 11.7c) Including a velocity boundary condition on the inflow

Figure 11.7d) Inlet velocity boundary condition indicated by arrows

8. Red arrows pointing in the right direction appears indicating the inlet velocity boundary condition, see figure 11.7d). Right click in the graphics window and select **Zoom/Pan/Rotate>>** **Zoom to Fit**. Right click again in the graphics window and select **Rotate View** once again to rotate the part so that the inner right surface is visible in the graphics window. Right click and click on **Select**. Right click on **Boundary Conditions** in the **Flow Simulation analysis tree** and select **Insert Boundary Condition…**. Click on the outlet boundary, see figure 11.8a). Click on the **Pressure Openings** button in the **Type** portion of the **Boundary Condition** window and select **Static Pressure**. Click OK to exit the window. If you zoom in on the outlet boundary you will see blue arrows indicating the static pressure boundary condition, see figure 11.8b).

Figure 11.8a) Selection of static pressure as boundary condition at the outlet of the flow region

Figure 11.8b) Outlet static pressure boundary condition

9. Insert the following boundary conditions: Ideal Wall for the upper wall and lower wall at the inflow region, see figures 11.9a) and 11.9b). These will be adiabatic and frictionless walls.

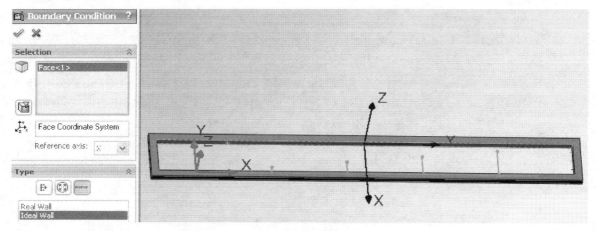

Figure 11.9a) Ideal wall boundary condition for upper wall

Figure 11.9b) Ideal wall boundary condition for lower wall at the inflow region

10. The last boundary condition will be in the form of a real wall. We will study the development of the thermal boundary layer on this wall. Set the temperature of the wall to **393.2 K**.

Figure 11.10 Real wall boundary condition for the flat plate

Inserting Goals

11. Right click on **Goals** in the **Flow Simulation analysis tree** and select **Insert Global Goals…**. Select **Min, Av** and **Max Temperature of Fluid** as global goals.

Figure 11.11a) Inserting global goals   Figure 11.11b) Selection of temperature of fluid

Running the Calculations for Low Reynolds Number

12. Select **Flow Simulation>>Solve>>Run** to start calculations. Click on the **Run** button in the **Run** window.

Figure 11.12a) Starting calculations

Figure 11.12b) Run window

Figure 11.12c) Solver window

Inserting Cut Plots

13. Right click on ⬖ Cut Plots in the 🔘 **Flow Simulation analysis tree** and select **Insert….**
Select the **Front Plane** from the 🔖 **FeatureManager design tree**. Click on [View Settings...].
Slide the **Number of colors:** slide bar to **101**. Select **Temperature** from the **Parameter** drop
down menu. Click on [OK]. Click OK ✓ to exit the **Cut Plot** window. Figures
11.13a) and 11.13b) shows the temperature gradient close to the heated wall of the flat plate.

Figure 11.13a) Thermal boundary layer along the flat plate

Figure 11.13b) Thermal boundary layer close to the wall

Plotting Temperature Profiles using Template

14. Place the file **"xy-plot figure 11.14c)"** into the **Local Disk (C:)/Program Files/SolidWorks (2)/SolidWorks Flow Simulation /lang/english/template/XY-plots** folder to make it available in the **Template** list. Click on the **FeatureManager design tree**. Click on the sketch **x = 0.2, 0.4, 0.6, 0.8 m**. Click on the **Flow Simulation analysis tree** tab. Right click **XY Plot** and select **Insert….** Check the **Temperature** box. Open the **Resolution** portion of the **XY Plot** window and slide the **Geometry Resolution** as far as it goes to the right. Click on the **Evenly Distribute Output Points** button and increase the number of points to **500**. Open the **Options** portion and check the **Display boundary layer** box. Select the template **"xy-plot figure 11.14c)"** from the drop down menu. Click OK to exit the **XY Plot** window. An Excel file will open with a graph of the temperature in the boundary layer at different streamwise positions, see figure 11.14c).

Figure 11.14a) Selecting the sketch for the XY Plot

Figure 11.14b) Settings for the XY plot

Figure 11.14c) Boundary layer temperature profiles on a flat plate at different streamwise positions

Theory

15. We now want to compare the temperature profiles with the theoretical temperature profile for laminar flow on a flat plate. First, we have to normalize the temperature T in the boundary layer

$$\Theta = \frac{T - T_\infty}{T_w - T_\infty} \qquad (1)$$

where T_∞ is the temperature in the free stream and T_w is the wall temperature. We also have to transform the wall normal coordinate into the similarity coordinate for comparison with the theoretical profile. The similarity coordinate is described by

$$\eta = y \sqrt{\frac{U}{vx}} \qquad (2)$$

where y (m) is the wall normal coordinate, U (m/s) is the free stream velocity, x (m) is the distance from the leading edge and v (m²/s) is the kinematic viscosity of the fluid. The fluid properties are evaluated at the film temperature $T_f = (T_w + T_\infty)/2$.

Plotting Non-dimensional Temperature Profiles using Template

Place the file **"xy-plot figure 11.15b)"** into the **Local Disk (C:)/Program Files/SolidWorks (2)/SolidWorks Flow Simulation /lang/english/template/XY-plots** folder to make it available in the **Template** list. Repeat step 14 and select the new template for the XY-plot.

Figure 11.15a) Selection of new template for XY-Plot

We see in figure 11.15b) that all profiles at different streamwise positions approximately collapse on the same curve when we use the boundary layer similarity coordinate.

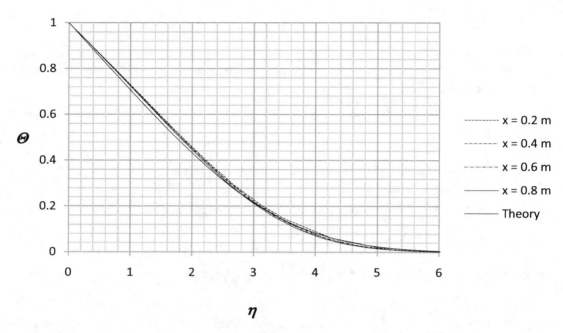

Figure 11.15b) Temperature profiles in comparison with the theoretical profile (full line)

The Reynolds number for the flow on a flat plate is defined as

$$Re_x = \frac{Ux}{\nu}$$
(3)

The Reynolds number varies between $Re = 50,100$ at $x = 0.2$ m and $Re = 200,400$ at $x = 0.8$ m. We now want to study how the local Nusselt number varies along the plate. It is defined as the local convection coefficient h_x times the streamwise coordinate x divided by the thermal conductivity k:

$$Nu_x = \frac{h_x x}{k}$$
(4)

The theoretical local Nusselt number for laminar flow is given by

$$Nu_x = 0.332 Pr^{1/3} Re_x^{1/2} \qquad Pr > 0.6$$
(5)

and for turbulent flow

$$Nu_x = 0.0296 Pr^{1/3} Re_x^{4/5} \qquad 5 \cdot 10^5 \leq Re_x \leq 10^7, 0.6 \leq Pr \leq 60$$
(6)

Plotting Local Nusselt Number using Template

16. Place the file **"xy-plot figure 11.16b)"** into the **Local Disk (C:)/Program Files/SolidWorks (2)/SolidWorks Flow Simulation /lang/english/template/XY-plots** folder to make it available in the **Template** list. Repeat step 14 but this time choose the sketch **x = 0 – 0.9 m** and check the box for **Heat Transfer Coefficient**. Select the new template, see figure 11.16a). An Excel file will open with a graph of the local Nusselt number versus the Reynolds number and compared with theoretical values for laminar thermal boundary layer flow, see figure 11.16b.

Figure 11.16a) Selection of another template for XY plot

Figure 11.16b) Local Nusselt number as a function of the Reynolds number

Running the Calculations for High Reynolds Number

17. In the next step, we will change the fluid to water in order to get higher Reynolds numbers. Start by selecting **Flow Simulation>>General Settings…** from the SolidWorks menu. Click on **Fluids** in the **Navigator** portion and click on the **Remove** button. Answer **OK** to the question that appears. Select **Water** from the **Liquids** and **Add** it as the **Project Fluid**. Change the **Flow type** to **Laminar and Turbulent**, see figure 11.17b). Close the **General Setting** window.

Figure 11.17a) Selection of general settings

Figure 11.17b) Selection of fluid and flow type

18. Right click the **Static Pressure Boundary Condition** in the **Flow Simulation analysis tree** and select **Edit Definition…**. Select **Turbulent Boundary Layer** in the **Boundary Layer** portion of the **Boundary Condition** window. Click **OK** ✓ to exit the **Boundary Condition** window. Right click the **Inlet Velocity Boundary Condition** in the **Flow Simulation analysis tree** and select **Edit Definition…**. Select **Laminar Boundary Layer**. Click **OK** ✓ to exit the **Boundary Condition** window. Right click the **Real Wall Boundary Condition** in the **Flow Simulation analysis tree** and select **Edit Definition…**. Set the temperature of the wall to **353.2 K**. Click **OK** ✓ to exit the **Boundary Condition** window.

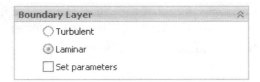

Figure 11.18 Selection of laminar boundary layer for inlet

19. Select **Flow Simulation** >>**Solve**>>**Run** to start calculations. Check the **Mesh** box and select **New Calculation**. Click on the **Run** button in the **Run** window.

Figure 11.19a) Creation of mesh and starting a new calculation

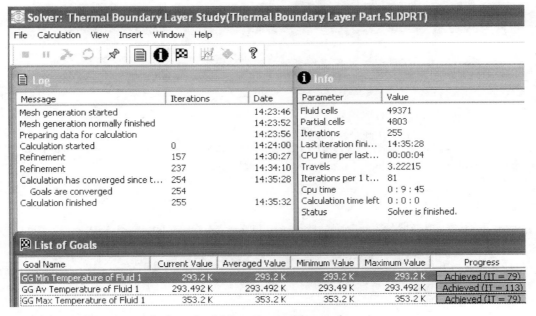

Figure 11.19b) Solver window for higher Reynolds number

20. Place the file **"xy-plot figure 11.20"** into the **Local Disk (C:)/Program Files/SolidWorks (2)/SolidWorks Flow Simulation /lang/english/template/XY-plots** folder to make it available in the **Template** list. Repeat step 16 but choose the template **"xy-plot figure 11.20"**. An Excel file will open with a graph of the local Nusselt number versus the Reynolds number and compared with theoretical values for laminar and turbulent thermal boundary layer flow, see figure 11.20.

Figure 11.20 is showing the Flow Simulation is able to capture the local Nusselt number in the laminar region in the Reynolds number range 60,000 – 380,000. At the critical Reynolds number Re_{cr} = 380,000 there is an abrupt increase in the Nusselt number caused by laminar to turbulent transition. In the turbulent region the Nusselt number is increasing again with a higher slope than in the laminar region.

Figure 11.20 Comparison between Flow Simulation (dashed line) and theoretical laminar and empirical turbulent local Nusselt numbers

The average Nusselt number Nu over the entire length L of the plate for laminar flow is given by

$$Nu = 0.664 Pr^{1/3} Re_L^{1/2} \qquad\qquad Pr > 0.6, \; Re_L \leq 5 \cdot 10^5 \qquad\qquad (7)$$

and for turbulent flow

$$Nu = 0.037 Pr^{1/3} Re_L^{4/5} \qquad 5 \cdot 10^5 \leq Re_L \leq 10^7, 0.6 \leq Pr \leq 60 \qquad (8)$$

If the boundary layer is laminar on one part of the plate and turbulent on the remaining part the average Nusselt number is determined by

$$Nu = \left[0.664 \sqrt{Re_{cr}} + 0.037 \left(Re_L^{4/5} - Re_{cr}^{4/5} \right) \right] Pr^{1/3} \qquad\qquad (9)$$

References

[1] Çengel Y.A., Heat Transfer: A Practical Approach, 2nd Edition, 2003.

[2] Schlichting H. and Gersten K., Boundary Layer Theory, 8th Revised and Enlarged Edition, Springer, 2001.

[3] SolidWorks Flow Simulation 2009 Technical Reference

[4] White, F. M., Fluid Mechanics, 4th Edition, McGraw-Hill, 1999.

Exercises

1. Change the number of cells per X and Y, see figure 11.6b) for the laminar boundary layer and plot graphs of the local Nusselt number versus Reynolds number for different combinations of cells per X and Y. Compare with theoretical results.

2. Modify the length of the heated section so that there is an unheated starting length and the heated section starts at $x = 0.4$ m. You get a cold real wall section for the part upstream of $x = 0.4$ m with the same temperature as the free stream temperature. Use cut plots and XY-Plots for temperature profiles in Flow Simulation to study the development of the thermal boundary layer on the flat plate.

3. Modify the length of the heated section so that it ends at x = 0.6 m and you get a cold real wall section for the remaining part of the plate with the same temperature as the free stream temperature. Use cut plots and XY-Plots for temperature profiles in Flow Simulation to study the development of the thermal boundary layer after the heated section.

Notes:

Chapter 12   Free-Convection on a Vertical Plate and from a Horizontal Cylinder

Objectives

- Setting up Flow Simulation projects for external flow
- Creating goals
- Running the calculations
- Using cut plots, XY plots from templates and animations to visualize the resulting flow fields
- Compare Flow Simulation results with theoretical and empirical data

Problem Description

We will use Flow Simulation to study the thermal two-dimensional laminar flow on a vertical flat plate and compare with the theoretical boundary layer solution. We will be using air as the fluid for the flow calculations. The temperature of the vertical hot wall will be set to 296.2 K while the temperature of the surrounding air is 293.2 K. We will determine temperature and velocity profiles and plot the same profiles using similarity variables. The variation of the local Nusselt number will be determined. We will also look at free convection from a heated cylinder in air. The diameter of the cylinder is 20 mm and the temperature of the same cylinder will be set to 393.2 K.

Figure 12.0 Thermal boundary layers on a vertical wall and around a horizontal cylinder

Setting up the Flow Simulation Project

1. Open the part named "**Free-Convection Boundary Layer Part**".

Figure 12.1 SolidWorks model for free-convection boundary layer

2. If Flow Simulation is not available in the menu, you have to add it from SolidWorks menu: **Tools>>Add Ins…** and check the corresponding **SolidWorks Flow Simulation** box. Select **Flow Simulation>>Project>>Wizard** to create a new Flow Simulation project. Create a new figuration named "**Free-Convection Boundary Layer Study**". Click on the **Next >** button. Select the default **SI (m-kg-s)** unit system and click on the **Next>** button once again.

Figure 12.2a) Starting a new Flow Simulation project

Figure 12.2b) Creating a name for the project

3. Use the **External Analysis type** and check the box for **Gravity** as **Physical Feature**. Click on the **Next >** button.

Figure 12.3 Analysis type window

4. Select **Air** from the **Gases** and add it as **Project Fluid**. Select **Laminar Only** from the **Flow Type** drop down menu. Click on the **Next >** button. Select **Wall temperature** from the **Default wall thermal condition Value** drop down menu. Set the **Wall temperature** to **296.2 K**. Click on the **Next >** button. Use default values for **Initial and Ambient Conditions**. Click on the **Next >** button. Slide the **Result resolution** to **8**. Click on the **Finish** button.

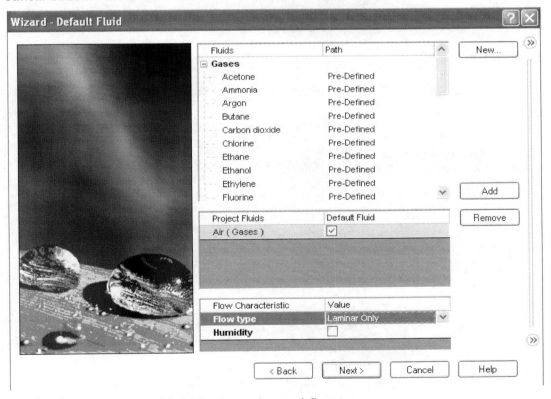

Figure 12.4a) Selection of fluid for the project and flow type

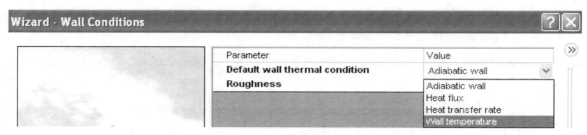

Figure 12.4b) Selection of wall temperature as thermal condition

Figure 12.4c) Wall temperature setting

5. Select **Flow Simulation>>Computational Domain…**. Click on the **Boundary Condition** tab and select **XY-Plane Flow** from the drop down menu. Click on the **Size** tab and set the size of the computational domain as shown in figure 12.5c). Click on the **OK** button to exit the **Computational Domain** window.

Figure 12.5a) Modifying the computational domain

Figure 12.5b) Selecting two dimensional flow condition

Figure 12.5c) Size of computational domain

6. Select **Flow Simulation>>Initial Mesh…**. Uncheck the **Automatic setting** box at the bottom of the window. Change both the **Number of cells per X:** to **200** and the **Number of cells per Y:** to **196**. Click on the **OK** button to exit the **Initial Mesh** window.

Figure 12.6a) Modifying the initial mesh

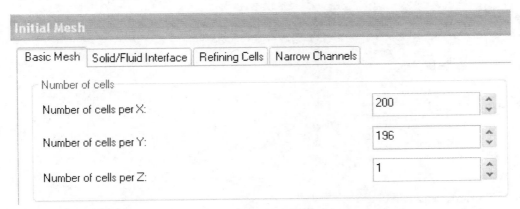

Figure 12.6b) Changing the number of cells in both directions

Inserting Goals

7. Open the **Input Data** folder and right click on **Goals** in the **Flow Simulation analysis tree** and select **Insert Global Goals…**. Select global goals as shown in figure 12.7b).

Figure 12.7a) Inserting global goals   Figure 12.7b) Selection of temperature of fluid

Running Calculations

8. Select **Flow Simulation>>Solve>>Run** to start calculations. Click on the **Run** button in the **Run** window.

Figure 12.8a) Starting calculations

Figure 12.8b) Run window

Figure 12.8c) Solver window

Inserting Cut Plots

9. Right click on Cut Plots in the Flow Simulation analysis tree and select Insert…. Select the Front Plane from the FeatureManager design tree. Click on View Settings… . Slide the Number of colors: slide bar to 254. Select Temperature from the Parameter drop down menu. Click on OK . Click OK to exit the Cut Plot window. Figure12.9a) shows the temperature distribution along the vertical wall and figure 12.9b) shows the velocity distribution.

Figure 12.9a) Thermal boundary layer   Figure 12.9b) Velocity boundary layer

Plotting Temperature and Velocity Profiles using Templates

10. Place the files "**xy-plot figure 12.10c)**" and "**xy-plot figure 12.10d)**" into the **Local Disk (C:)/Program Files/SolidWorks (2)/SolidWorks Flow Simulation/ /lang/english/template/XY-plots** folder to make it available in the **Template** list. Click on the FeatureManager design tree. Click on the sketch **y = 0.2, 0.4, 0.6, 0.8 m**. Click on the Flow Simulation analysis tree tab. Right click **XY Plot** and select **Insert…**. Check the **Temperature** box. Open the **Resolution** portion of the **XY Plot** window and slide the **Geometry**

Resolution as far as it goes to the right. Click on the **Evenly Distribute Output Points** button and increase the number of points to **500**. Open the **Options** portion and check the **Display boundary layer** box. Select the template "**xy-plot figure 12.10c)**" from the drop down menu. Click OK ✔ to exit the **XY Plot** window. An Excel file will open with a graph of the temperature in the boundary layer, see figure 12.10c). Repeat this step and select template "**xy-plot figure 12.10d)**" and **Y-velocity** for the XY-plot, see figure 12.10d).

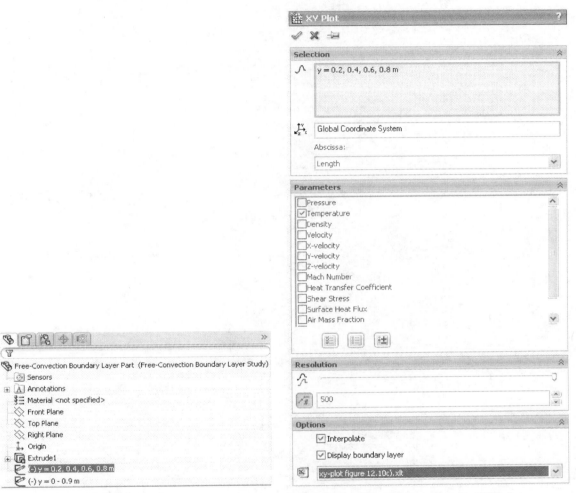

Figure 12.10a) Selecting the sketch   Figure 12.10b) Settings for the XY plot

Figure 12.10c) Boundary layer temperature profiles on a vertical heated flat plate.

Figure 12.10d) Boundary layer velocity profiles on a vertical heated flat plate.

Theory

11. We now want to compare the temperature and velocity profiles with the theoretical profiles. First, we have to normalize the temperature T in the boundary layer

$$\Theta = \frac{T - T_\infty}{T_w - T_\infty} \tag{1}$$

where T_∞ is the ambient temperature and T_w is the wall temperature. We also have to transform the wall normal coordinate into the similarity coordinate for comparison with the theoretical profile. The similarity coordinate is described by

$$\eta = \frac{x}{y} Ra^{1/4} \qquad\qquad Ra = \frac{\beta g (T_w - T_\infty) y^3}{\alpha v} \tag{2}$$

where Ra is the Rayleigh number, x is the wall normal coordinate, y is the coordinate along the vertical wall, g is acceleration due to gravity, α is the thermal diffusivity, β is the coefficient of volume expansion and v is the kinematic viscosity of the fluid. The fluid properties are evaluated at the film temperature $T_f = (T_w + T_\infty)/2$. The theoretical velocity component v in the y direction is given by

$$v = -\frac{\alpha}{y} Ra^{1/2} f' \tag{3}$$

and there are two nonlinear coupled differential equations for f and Θ

$$4\text{Pr}\,(f''' - \Theta) - 3ff'' + 2f'^2 = 0 \qquad\qquad 4\Theta'' - 3\Theta'f = 0 \tag{4}$$

where Pr is the Prandtl number. We have the following boundary conditions

$$f(0) = f'(0) = f'(\infty) = 0 \qquad\qquad \Theta(0) = 1, \Theta(\infty) = 0 \tag{5}$$

Plotting Non-dimensional Temperature and Velocity Profiles using Templates

Place the files **"xy-plot figure 12.11b)"** and **"xy-plot figure 12.11c)"** into the **Local Disk (C:)/Program Files/SolidWorks (2)/SolidWorks Flow Simulation/ /lang/english/template/XY-plots** folder to make it available in the **Template** list. Repeat step 10 and select the new templates for the XY-plots.

Figure 12.11a) Selection of new template for XY-Plot

We see in figure 12.11b) that all profiles at different streamwise positions approximately collapse on the same curve when we use the boundary layer similarity coordinate. For the theoretical velocity maximum in figure 12.11c) the maximum is slightly lower than Flow Simulation results.

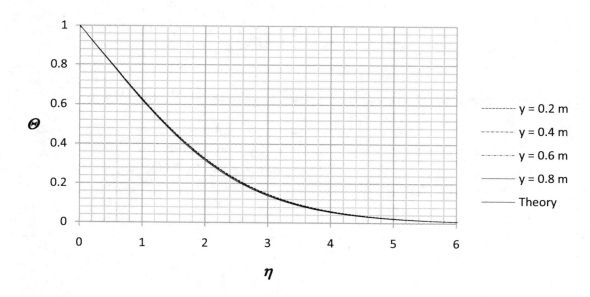

Figure 12.11b) Temperature profiles in comparison with the theoretical profile (full line)

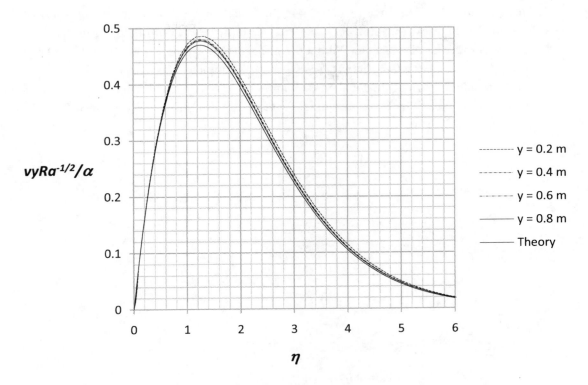

Figure 12.11c) Velocity profiles in comparison with the theoretical profile (full line)

We now want to study how the local Nusselt number varies along the vertical plate. It is defined as the local convection coefficient h_y times the vertical coordinate y divided by the thermal conductivity k:

$$Nu_y = \frac{h_y y}{k} \qquad (6)$$

A curve-fit formula for local Nusselt number for laminar free-convection flow on a vertical flat wall is given by Churchill and Usagi

$$Nu_y = \frac{0.503 Ra^{1/4}}{[1+\left(\frac{0.492}{Pr}\right)^{\frac{9}{16}}]^{4/9}} \qquad 10^5 < Ra < 10^9 \qquad (7)$$

The overall Nusselt number for free-convection flow on a vertical plate is given by Churchill and Chu

$$Nu_L^{1/2} = 0.825 + \frac{0.387 Ra_L^{1/6}}{[1+\left(\frac{0.492}{Pr}\right)^{\frac{9}{16}}]^{8/27}} \qquad Ra_L \le 10^{12} \qquad (8)$$

Plotting Local Nusselt Number using Template

12. Place the file **"xy-plot figure 12.12b)"** into the **Local Disk (C:)/Program Files/SolidWorks (2)/SolidWorks Flow Simulation/ /lang/english/template/XY-plots** folder to make it available in the **Template** list. Repeat step 10 but this time choose the sketch **y = 0 – 0.9 m** and check the box for **Heat Transfer Coefficient**. Select the new template, see figure 12.12a). An Excel file will open with a graph of the local Nusselt number versus the Rayleigh number and compared with empirical curve-fit values for laminar free-convection flow on a vertical wall, see figure 12.12b).

Figure 12.12a) Selection of another template for XY plot

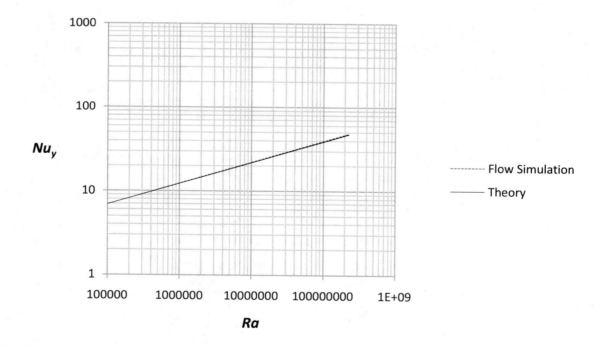

Figure 12.12b) Local Nusselt number as a function of the Rayleigh number

Free Convection from a Horizontal Cylinder

13. Open the file named "**Free-Convection from a Cylinder**". Select **Flow Simulation>>Calculation Control Options…** , click on the **Saving** tab and check the **Value** box for **Periodic Saving**. Click on the plus sign next to **Periodic Saving** and enter **2** for the **Period**. Click on the **OK** button to exit the **Calculation Control Options** window. Select **Flow Simulation>>General Settings…**, click on **Analysis type** in the **Navigator** and make sure that the **Time-dependent** value box is checked for **Physical Features**. Click on **Fluids** in the **Navigator** and make sure that **Laminar and Turbulent** is selected for **Flow type** under **Flow Characteristic**.

Select **Flow Simulation>>Solve>>Run** to start calculations. Click on the **Run** button in the **Run** window. Select **Flow Simulation>>Results>>Load/Unload Results**. Repeat this step if the Load Results window does not open. Click on the **Open** button to load the results. Repeat step 9 to create cut plots for the temperature field and the velocity field around the cylinder, see figures 12.13b) and 12.13c).

Figure 12.13a) Solver window for free-convection from a cylinder

Figure 12.13b) Temperature field around cylinder   Figure 12.13c) Velocity field from cylinder

Animating the Temperature Field for the Cylinder

14. We now want to animate the cut plots for the temperature field. Right click on the cut plot for temperature and select **Animate....** Click on **More...** to expand the animation controls section, see figure 12.14a). Click on the control point for **Animation 1** at 00:10 and drag it towards 00:00, see figure 12.14b). Select the animation wizard, see figure 12.14c). Use the default animation time of **10 s** and click on the **Next>** button. Click on the **Next>** button in following window. Check the **Scenario** animation type and click on the **Next>** button. **Start from: 0 s** and **Finish at 10.3352 s**. Click on the **Finish** button to exit the animation wizard. Click on the right control point for **Temperature** located close to 0 s and drag it to 10.4 s, see figure 12.14d). Click on the

▷ **Play** button to start the animation. Exit animation 1. Repeat this step and create an animation for the velocity field.

Figure 12.14a) Animation controls

Figure 12.14b) Moving of an animation control point

Figure 12.14c) Animation wizard

Figure 12.14d) Moving the right control point for temperature

References

[1] Bejan A., Convection Heat Transfer, 3rd Edition, Wiley, 2004.

[2] Sparrow E.M., Husar R.B. and Goldstein R.J., Observations and other characteristics of thermals. *J. Fluid Mech.,* **42**, 465 – 470, 1970.

[3] White F. M., Viscous Fluid Flow, 2nd Edition, McGraw-Hill, 1991.

Exercises

1. Use Flow Simulation to study two-dimensional free-convection interaction between four heated horizontal cylinders arranged in a staggered grid, see figure E1. Make cut plots and animations of the temperature and velocity fields from the cylinders. Use a cylinder diameter of 20 mm and set the surface temperature of each cylinder to 393.2 K. Use air as the fluid. Set the center distance between the horizontal cylinders to H = 30 mm and the center distance between the vertical cylinders V = 60 mm.

Figure E1 Geometry for staggered grid of four horizontal cylinders

2. Use Flow Simulation to study free-convection on a vertical cylinder in air with a diameter of 20 mm and a length of 1 m. Set the surface temperature to 300 K and determine temperature and velocity profiles at different locations along cylinder.

3. Use Flow Simulation to study two-dimensional, time-dependent free-convection from a horizontal flat plate, use a 1 m wide plate but choose your own thickness of the plate. Set the temperature and roughness of the plate to different values and make cut plots and animations of the temperature and velocity fields in water to see if you can get Flow Simulation to generate intermittent rise of thermals as shown in experiments by Sparrow at al.[2]

Index

A

B

I

Notes: